C000084056

THE JEWISH GUIDE TO
ADULTERY

Other books by this author:

Dating Secrets of the Ten Commandments
(Hodder & Stoughton Ltd, 1999)

Dreams
(Bash Publications Inc., 1991)

An Intelligent Person's Guide to Judaism
(Duckworth, 1999)

Kosher Sex:
A recipe for passion and intimacy
(New edition:
Hodder & Stoughton Ltd, 1999)

Moses of Oxford:
A Jewish vision of a university and its life,
volumes 1 and 2
(André Deutsch Publishers Ltd, 1994)

Wisdom, Understanding and Knowledge
(Jason Aronson Inc., 1996)

The Wolf Shall Lie with the Lamb
(Jason Aronson, Inc., 1993)

Wrestling with the Divine:
A Jewish response to suffering
(Jason Aronson Inc., 1995)

THE JEWISH GUIDE TO
ADULTERY

HOW TO TURN YOUR MARRIAGE
INTO A DELICIOUS AFFAIR

SHMULEY BOTEACH

Hodder & Stoughton
LONDON SYDNEY AUCKLAND

Copyright © 1999 by Shmuley Boteach

First published in Great Britain in 1995

This revised edition first published in 1999

The right of Shmuley Boteach to be identified as the Author of
the Work has been asserted by him in accordance
with the Copyright, Designs and Patents Act 1988.

10 9 8 7 6 5 4 3 2 1

All rights reserved. No part of this publication may be
reproduced, stored in a retrieval system, or transmitted,
in any form or by any means without the prior written
permission of the publisher, nor be otherwise circulated
in any form of binding or cover other than that in which
it is published and without a similar condition being
imposed on the subsequent purchaser.

ISBN 0 340 74558 4

Typeset by Avon Dataset Ltd, Bidford-on-Avon, Warks

Printed and bound in Great Britain by
Clays Ltd, St Ives plc

Hodder and Stoughton Ltd
A Division of Hodder Headline PLC
338 Euston Road
London NW1 3BH

For Debbie

Contents

Acknowledgements

With this, the second edition of *The Jewish Guide to Adultery*, I must first offer heartfelt thanks to my editors at Hodder and Stoughton for agreeing to reissue this book. At first, when Judith Longman and Charles Nettleton told me that they would re-edit the book for republication, I must admit that I was very worried. After all, how do you improve on perfection? As if it were an expert Michaelangelo sculpture, I was wary of them taking their hammers and chisels to my masterpiece. And yet, they insisted that the book be cut down by half. Being of a compromising nature, I was prepared to meet them halfway and agreed to delete my middle initial from the book jacket. But nothing satisfies these two, even this great sacrifice. A compromise was finally reached when we agreed simply to remove every occurrence of the word 'I' or 'me'. After this, the book needed no further editing, having been reduced by over one thousand pages. Nevertheless, any imperfections in this book must therefore be attributed to Judith and Charles only who had the temerity to mess with the supernal wisdom as it embodied itself in a paperback. The mistakes are theirs, the good stuff entirely my own. The actual perpetrator of the hatchet job was Penny Phillips. I tried calling her many times to spare some of the book's profound prose but she was always asleep, complaining that remaining awake while reading the book was proving impossible.

I have to admit that I had another fear in allowing

this book to be reissued. Central to the Jewish religion is the belief in freedom of choice. God does not want robots or automatons worshipping Him. He therefore grants us the power to choose our own way in life. We may even choose to live outside His will. But the arguments in favour of marriage, fidelity, and indeed a life of holiness in sex and relationships within this book are so strong and so persuasive that it immediately removes the possibility of anyone exercising their choice to act contrary to the divine will. As one of my friends said to me, 'Shmuley, your logic is so strong that it is like holding a howitzer loaded with explosive common sense to someone's head. How can they disagree with you?' I therefore initially thought it unfair to publish the book again, as this would immediately bring about a world devoid of sin and perversion. But then, the thought of extra cash served as a strong counter-argument, and I gave in to Judith and Charles's begging for the copyright.

I would like to thank my good friend and agent, Vivienne Schuster, for her expert negotiations on my behalf. At first I could not believe that she had secured the one-figure deal, plus a six-pack of Foster's, for the book. Only she could have persuaded Hodder to so vastly overpay. But then she really outdid herself, securing a further £1 million as a bonus. And all I had to do was sign a contract saying that I would move to Rangoon and never contact Charles and Judith again. And all along, I thought they were unreasonable.

I also wish to extend my appreciation to Chrissy Iley, whose *Sunday Times* article on this book led to its original publication. Chrissy has since gone on to far better and greater things, indeed real stardom as one of Britain's premier feature writers and columnists. But she still hasn't forgotten me and has remained a very close friend. Indeed, occasionally she will even get her secretary's cleaning lady to return my calls. But as an American still striving to understand British collo-quialisms, I'm still not sure what 'Piss off' exactly means. Is Chrissy inviting me to use the lavatories at her home?

This book was originally plagiarized . . . uh, er, I mean, *created* from the hundreds of hours I have spent counselling and serving as an ear to the complaints and thoughts that people have about their marriages and relationships. I am most grateful to the many people who flattered me by taking me into their confidence. We all inhabit this planet together and we humans find ample occasion to lean on one another. Far from this being a sign of weakness, the need for human friend-ship, warmth and advice is the key to fraternity and brotherhood. But in order for this to be effective, there must first be trust. And confidentiality, which I guard most zealously, is the essence of trust. I therefore want to thank all those who trusted me with their personal lives and intimate details of their relationships. In appreciation, I have included small photographs of them adjacent to their respective stories along with their home phone numbers and e-mail addresses.

If I were to be asked what my great blessing is, without any hesitation I would of course say that it is my laptop computer. A close second, however, is my wife Debbie. My wife is devoted and loving to me in a manner I find almost impossible to reciprocate, which is why I don't even try and make the effort, preferring to love myself instead. Debbie is always there to gently goad me to ever higher rungs of achievement. There is a certain tenderness in the way she always says, 'Hey Shmuck, get your smelly feet off the sofa, turn off the television, and get your lazy *tochas* back to the computer and write something that doesn't embarrass us both.'

Still, any beautiful insight I have learned into the mystery of human relationships I have discovered with her at my side. Her sixth sense which penetrates far deeper than my own more superficial view of love has made so many things more understandable – such as why she refuses to spend any time with me – and in this sense this book is as much hers as it is mine (otherwise known as guilt by association). Together, we are blessed, thank God, with six beautiful children and two mothers-in-law.

Finally, I thank the benevolent Creator for His infinite kindness and love toward me, of which I have never felt myself worthy. God has always watched over and protected me. I can only hope that I will always be a worthy exemplar of Jewish values. Of course, there is about as much chance of that happening as the Pope converting to Judaism. (Well, he already has the yarmulka, so you never know.)

I close, dear reader, with a prayer and a request. Help make the world a better place. Go out and buy another copy of my book.

Shmuley Boteach
Oxford and London, England
January, 1999

Foreword

'Personally I know nothing about sex because I've always been married.'
Zsa Zsa Gabor, 'Sayings of the Week', *Observer*,
16 August 1987

The main reason for my undertaking this study has to do specifically with the fact that I am a Rabbi. If there is one thing that I have always sought both as a religious thinker and as a religious individual it is the synthesis of heaven and earth. What I mean by this is to lead the kind of life in which religious teaching on the one hand, and the experiences and truisms of everyday life on the other, are not only compatible, but identical. I have always believed that if the teachings of heaven cannot be corroborated, or even discovered, through everyday living, then not only may we question their validity and authenticity, but worse, they are totally irrelevant to man. If God has nothing to say to man that actually works, and that he can actually verify with his own heart and mind, then His teaching might just as soon remain only in the heavens where it can benefit the angels and disembodied creatures, rather than descending to earth and confounding man. You may well ask, 'What is a Rabbi doing writing a book on adultery?' This book is a serious attempt at helping to

1

make marriages work by addressing the biggest marital problem of all: the loss of passion in monogamous relationships.

And this is where, ironically, the subject of adultery comes in. Adultery serves as one of the bridges between the religious and secular worlds: even the most rabid secularists agree that adultery is wrong and that the pain that it causes is among the most severe to be found in any area of life. While the attitude towards so many other forms of human behaviour is still being debated between religionists and secularists, on the subject of adultery they are (nearly) all in agreement.

When I was eight years old, my parents separated. Try as they might, and they certainly made a go of it, they simply could not live together. A combination of radically different upbringing, social and financial backgrounds, and plain stubbornness made their life together less than peaceful and pleasurable (to use the British understatement). They ended up parting, and it was difficult for everyone involved, especially my brothers and sisters, since we were all very young at the time. And yet, even amidst my exposure to the acrimony of their marriage, I never gave up on the idea of marriage. In fact, I committed myself to trying not to repeat the same mistakes which they had made, and which were so readily apparent. I basically said to myself, 'Marriage is a good thing. My parents, however, didn't go about it in the right way. The problem was with the *individuals* and not with the *institution*.'

After my parents divorced we moved from Los Angeles to Miami Beach and I was transported into a far more affluent Jewish neighbourhood and day school. I found myself perfectly at home because there were very many other kids in my class whose parents had divorced. Still smarting from the effects of my parents' divorce, I felt an immediate camaraderie and kinship with these children and befriended them easily. It was when I began frequenting their homes that I noticed that we had nothing in common at all. Sure, their parents were divorced too. But they were the best of friends. Their fathers came to their homes and sat and joked with their mothers. They got along fine. They had simply lost interest in each other. They had fallen out of love. They were no longer attracted or excited by one another. And so, whereas I always spoke with my friends in an endearing way about marriage, and often pontificated about whom I would marry, they did not. They had no time for it all, and when asked would almost swear that they would never marry. The reason was simple. They saw a flaw in the *institution* of marriage. Marriage did not work. Monogamy did not work. People simply could not stay married and interested in each other for long stretches of time.

Friendship after divorce?

When people say to me that the way my parents divorced, and the acrimony that still exists between them, are wrong, I disagree with them vehemently. I say I don't want my parents pretending they once were not married. I don't want them speaking as if they are mere friends. I don't want them acting as though what they shared was just casual. They were married, it was intense. Either it remains as intense as marriage or it doesn't exist at all. To pretend that your ex-wife can become your best friend, or to pretend in any marriage that if you are best friends that is good for the marriage, is rubbish. It destroys whatever chance we have in life for sustaining something intense. And while I agree with those who argue that divorced parents can at least be civil to each other for the sake of the children, civil and cordial do not mean friendly.

Any marriage that can become a casual friendship was never really intense. Divorced couples should break completely. They should find it difficult to converse. They should harbour negative feelings toward each other, because this is infinitely better than harbouring no feeling at all. Let them react and continue to believe that this thing they were once in was intense, so that they can have hope for success in their next marriage.

At my own wedding my parents could not even bring themselves to congratulate each other. I am often asked by friends whether that bothered me. 'Not at all,' I say. On the contrary, if they had sat and spoken together at the reception amicably, that would have bothered me. Because then I would forever have been asking the question, 'If you can get along so well right now the way you are, then why did you get divorced in the first place?' But since they cannot get along, I have my answer. They fought, therefore they divorced. It wasn't that their feelings for each other dissipated until they just drifted apart. Thus, I still have hope in marriage. It can remain intense. Just look. Even after so many years, my parents still feel all the hurt, pain, anger, and frustration. Because marriage is indeed intense, and those feelings never change.

Ever since my parents divorced, I have had a passion in life: to make marriages work again. I believe with all my heart and soul that man's first religious calling is not just to pray and recite hymns, but to help his fellow man lead a better, more joyous life. People do this in many different ways, and I have no greater wish than to make my contribution to humanity by helping husbands and wives to fall in love with each other all over again, and remain fully focused sexually on each other, rather than sharing intimacy with others outside the marriage.

Over the past few decades many self-help books have appeared with the express intention of restoring passion in marriage and enhancing the quality of married life. Where this book differs from its predecessors is this: whereas many of them deal with symptoms of problems, this book goes straight to the essence of those problems. Whereas what these other books offer is primarily *techniques*, this book offers a new state of mind.

Although, in their own way, many of these books are helpful, they ignore the central malady in today's marriage: husbands and wives are drifting apart. They appear to be bored with each other, and the monotony of their lives leads them to argue about trivialities, or avoid conversation altogether by digesting copious amounts of television. To rectify this situation, what is needed is a new way in which we look at and perceive our spouse, so that in our eyes they will always be seductive and exciting. We need to learn how to make love not just with our bodies, but with our *heads*.

If we can renew our sexual interest in our spouse, then many of the overt problems, like continuous bickering, will fall by the wayside. A great Jewish sage once said, 'When you have nothing to do, you end up doing what you ought not to do.' When we are bored with our spouse, when we feel we don't want to be married to them, we pick a quarrel on the silliest pretext. In this book you will see marriage, adultery, and sexual attraction in a completely new light, and learn how to rediscover passion in your marriage.

Why learn from adultery?

I begin with two very simple observations. First, there is a dramatic increase in extramarital affairs in the world today. Second, whereas husbands and wives, even if they love each other, can feel bored with having sex together, the same is not true of lovers involved in adulterous affairs. The sex life of the average husband and his mistress, or of a wife and her lover, never seems to dissipate in the way it might if they were married.

This book identifies what it is about adultery that makes it so exciting and irresistible to so many people; what it is about a new sexual partner that causes such passion; and what can be done to transpose those same feelings into marriage. In other words, it is designed to help you look upon the woman you married not just as your wife, but as your *mistress*, or to make the man to whom you were wed and whose bed you share become not just your husband, but your *lover*, to restore sex in your marriage to the central position it would occupy if you were having an extramarital affair. Looking forward to sharing intimacy with your husband or your wife, and having a satisfying sex life, is the essence of marriage. Nothing is more important. Our eyes should never turn to other men and women, because our marriage should be – and *can* be – so exciting that we will never want to stray.

The Catch-22 of marriage

Every marriage, every long-term relationship between a man and woman, involves an inherent Catch-22. The closer a husband and wife draw together in marriage, the more they fall in love with each other, the more familiar they become as well. The more they become 'best friends' (which is what some people portray as the ideal in marriage), the more they become tired or bored with each other, and almost inevitably their sex life will commensurably suffer.

That excitement and passion are gradually lost in marriage is a contention that I have never heard anyone disagree with. During the course of writing this book, I was invited to lecture on the subject in many countries, including South Africa, the United States, Germany, Australia, Norway, Sweden, Canada, and of course throughout the length and breadth of Britain. The lectures always contained something in the title about restoring passion to the dullness that is bound to ensue in marriage. Never once, in all my travels, did a member of the audience ever stand up and say, 'What the hell are you talking about? What monotony in marriage? That certainly hasn't happened to me.'

How do you overcome the lack of novelty in marriage, when you have the same sexual partner every time, and wake every morning to the same face? It's a major problem. How does a wife feel when she un-dresses at night, and her husband continues to read the newspaper? The very success of the marriage works against you if you become closely-knit. If you do everything together, tell each other every secret, share everything and enjoy each other's company, you also run the risk of losing the fire in your marriage. It is as if God has placed inherent imperfections in life. The more dedicated and devoted a spouse you are, the more it seems that your partner will fantasise about someone else's heretofore unexplored body. It is only if you embark on long periods of separation, and don't see each other very often, that you might long to be reunited physically.

The familiarity which marriage and monogamy create can mean that there is nothing left about you to conquer or discover. Your spouse can't embark on a journey of adventure with you because you are such a well-known quantity. But they can look upon a business colleague or new acquaintance who is known to them only in a superficial way and think, 'My, how inviting. Now wouldn't that be interesting!'

The good news is that a marriage *can* transcend this Catch-22, the apparent mutual exclusivity of familiarity and passion. I believe that marriage actually presents the greatest possibility for synthesising familiarity and passion, thus affording the opportunity of reaching the highest summits of sexual excitement and passion.

Chasing as many sexual partners as possible, having someone new in your bed every night, is not the answer. Admittedly, the novelty and constant change will probably not breed monotony or boredom. And yes, it probably will be passionate and exciting. But it will lack *familiarity and informality*. When a couple barely know each other and have sex, they are as focused on impressing each other each and demonstrating their sexual prowess as they are on enjoying themselves and making sure each other has a good time. They are also conscious of the fact that they, their bodies, and their performance, are being judged. They are so hell-bent on making sure that they score well that they simply cannot relax and be themselves. And so while the experience may be very passionate, it will not be as exciting as sharing the same experience with someone you love, who you know is not judging you, and with whom you can simply focus and be natural. The kind of sex that is totally spontaneous, uncontrived, instinctive and electric, that leaves you feeling far closer to your partner when the experience is over, is the kind of sex which can only be found through familiarity, closeness, long-term commitment and marriage.

The soul of adultery can invigorate the body of marriage

The only way to overcome the monotony that almost inevitably develops in a relationship is by ensuring that your marriage is as sexually exciting as it possibly can be. Don't worry for the moment about all the other problems that may exist in marriage – the bickering, the lack of respect, the needling. I believe firmly that if our sex lives become as inviting, exciting, and pleasurable as they once were, then all these other things will fall by the wayside. They may still exist, but they will melt into insignificance against a couple's satisfaction in the most important area of all: their intimate lives together.

Why else is it that trivia can be blown so completely

out of proportion in marriage, if not because those things which were once much more pleasurable are no longer so? How else can we explain why coming home to dinner on time can become more important than going to the bedroom and enjoying each other's touch? I have a close friend who is one of the leading divorce lawyers in Britain. She claims that over half her divorces are between men and women who complain that their partner is so untidy that they cannot live with them. Can you imagine husbands and wives leaving each other because they find each other too untidy! Do you believe that any of them are really more interested in always having a tidy home, a clean kitchen, no toothpaste smeared on the bathroom basin, than in having the most wonderful sex life together?

When a single man or woman is invited home by a member of the opposite sex for a nightcap, they don't first look around to check whether or not the room is tidy. They are interested in one thing, and one thing only, and that one thing is so inviting and so desirable that everything else falls into oblivion.

A one-night stand is, of course, radically different from a marriage, which is more about having to get on with someone in an everyday context. It may seem naive to say that if you have a great sex life nothing else matters. Nevertheless, I believe that one of the most prevalent modern-day fallacies is that successful marriage is more about *compatibility of interests* than anything else. If this is true, then homosexuality makes much more sense than heterosexuality, and men should marry men instead of women. After all, the average man or woman shares more in common with members of the same sex than with the opposite. The fact that when we marry we look forward to sharing a life with the opposite sex teaches us that marriage is primarily about *attraction*, rather than compatibility. And it is uniquely the power of a satisfying sex life that can transform the tedium of waking up to the same face and going to bed with the same body into a welcome experience.

This is the power of passion, and why it is so necessary. Those who marry do so because what they desire most is to share the same bed, not just the same house, with the person they love. What often occurs, unfortunately, is that later in the marriage shopping and cooking and earning a living become more important than intimacy, as the bedroom yields slowly to the kitchen, dining room and office as the focus of the couple's activity.

The cycle of adultery, even that of the wife, usually *begins* with the husband. Men innately desire (some would say require) many sexual partners and associate passion with newness. They may love their wives, but they still seek out new bodies. They become restless with the limitations of monogamy as their wives become too familiar to them to retain their excitement.

The monotony men begin to feel causes them to start ignoring their wives. In the worst cases, they forget their marital vows and actually pursue new excitement outside of marriage. But in either scenario, the wife feels neglected, undesirable and 'old'. She knows that her husband's mind is not on her, and so feels rejected. Whether or not her husband actually commits adultery is immaterial.

A wife therefore begins to yearn for the love and affection that existed at the outset of her marriage. If she is lucky, and both she and her husband work hard enough, their affection can be rekindled. But if she gives up hope, especially if she knows her husband's attentions to be on other women, she will either close up and become unhappy and embittered, or look outside the marriage herself.

Amidst the many useful ways of enriching marriage and preventing adultery to be found in this book, none is so important as the techniques by which to achieve passion and newness in marriage. A husband who can be taught always to see his wife in a passionate light will be able to cater to his natural disposition without repressing his essential sexual nature. The result will be that his wife will feel like the most desirable woman in the world. Both will abstain from adultery, not for religious or social reasons alone, but because they feel immensely happy and sexually satisfied.

It is to restoring the intimacy and eroticism of our marriages by examining the phenomenon of adultery that this book is dedicated. I seek to use adultery, or rather, *the possibility of adultery*, to give us the most exciting marriages. The possibility that even the most committed husbands and wives might stray is something beneficial in marriage. I am seeking to curb adultery not through religious diatribe and condemnation, but by making monogamy and marriage even more inviting and pleasurable.

Monogamy and the sin of adultery

The pain of adultery

When I had just turned 21, I returned to the United States from Australia where I had been a student for two years. I was sitting with a close married friend talking over old times in a hotel lounge in Manhattan, when a young couple walked in together, immediately catching everyone's attention because of the amount of noise they were making. The man, who had a handsome dark complexion and was dressed in the finest Italian suit, looked very suave and charismatic, and was quite obviously the quintessential 'ladies' man'. His wife, although attractive, looked dishevelled and distraught. They sat down at a table not far from us, and even if I had had no intention of eavesdropping on their conversation (and I was tempted), I could not have avoided it because of the way she shouted. 'You promised me never to speak to her again. How could you? After everything we've been through because of her, how could you smile at her and be so nice to her?' She was pounding on his chest. 'How could you? You promised. I thought she was out of our life for ever. And here you go and pull her right back in. How could you?'

Her husband, clasping both her hands in his, was trying desperately to calm her down. But it was not working. She was clearly very, very hurt and upset. He spoke to her quietly, caressing her cheek, not seeming to care whether or not people were listening. He was concerned only with consoling her. 'Honey, you know I love you. You know that she meant nothing to me. I promise. She's history.' He petted her softly as he spoke, kissed her on the lips, and it appeared as though she would forgive him. She allowed herself to drop softly into his arms, but then immediately she recoiled – and with a vengeance. She stood up, pounded her fists against his chest, and shouted even louder, 'No! I won't let you do this to me again. No, I won't forgive you. You *don't* love me. If you loved me you wouldn't do this to me.' And she pounded harder. They argued a bit more in this way, with her shrieking and crying and pounding his chest, amidst his futile attempts to calm and console her, and his promises of future fidelity.

What I remember most is the unconcealed pain on the woman's face; the frazzled hair, the long black mascara streaks down her cheeks. She was evidently hurt so badly that she was oblivious of the spectacle she was making of herself. She did not care about her appearance or about others' impression of her.

Her pain was something I could not understand. I was not yet married, nor had I ever had a serious girlfriend or even a casual relationship. In the Rabbinical seminaries (Yeshivot) I had attended, we were strictly single and celibate, and had very limited exposure to women. This kind of pain was incomprehensible to me. Had someone died, I asked myself? How could this possibly be so serious? The story was obvious. Her husband had been unfaithful to her, or at the very least had shown serious affection towards another woman. Yet his wife acted as though her husband was no longer living and she was in mourning for him.

After the episode was over, and my friend and I were both feeling guilty for eavesdropping, he sat staring silently and very thoughtfully into space. Our conversation had long since died, and I saw that suddenly he was not in the mood for talking. I interrupted his reverie to ask what he was thinking about. He turned to me slowly and spoke.

'What I have just witnessed has brought back terrible memories and made me think. Shmuley, you know that I've been married for three years now. I am fortunate in that I have a loving wife and we are very happy together. But in the first year of marriage, I was working very hard to build up my business and was keeping very late hours. After a few months, my commitment to my business became an outright abuse of the time I should have been spending with my wife. She begged me to give her more time. Every night she would ring and ask when I was coming home, and my response was always the same: just a few more minutes. Invariably she would give up on me at about 10 or 11 o'clock and go to sleep on her own. I felt that my neglect of my personal life was justified by the fact that I was at the early stages of building up my business, which was for both of us, and inevitably, because it was new, it was going to be difficult and very time-consuming. I was confident that after this stage was over, I would be free to spend all of my spare time with my wife. Therefore, I asked her to be patient. It wouldn't always be like this. At times I even accused her of selfishness and of having the luxury of taking it easy at night while I had to work hard for our mutual benefit.

'Well, after a while, I began to notice that she didn't wait for me to come home the way she once had. Her mind was not on me the way it had once been, either. She worked as a part-time librarian and I suspected that she was developing a liking for a co-worker, a very soft and friendly young man. She spoke about him constantly, and acted very unnatural around him when the three of us were together. One day, I confronted her and asked her what was going on. I never suspected anything improper; my wife was just not the type. After much denial, she confirmed that she had very warm feelings towards him, and she suspected that he felt the same towards her. She told me that nothing whatsoever had happened between them, but they usually ate lunch together in the cafeteria and had wonderful conversations together. Still, they had never discussed their mutual affection. But she did say that she was very attracted to him, often fantasised about him, and on several occasions had even dreamt about them kissing each other.

'I was devastated. I would gladly have traded the hurt and anguish I experienced on that evening for any form of physical pain, even though I knew that nothing sexual had taken place. I was lucky in that I was able to reverse the damage caused by my neglect by showing my wife extravagant love, attention, and affection. But I still believe that she harbours a special place in her heart for that man. Whenever I question her on the subject, she refuses to speak about it. And she still looks starry-eyed whenever he is mentioned. And if we occasionally bump into him, she cannot be herself but becomes very self-conscious. I just wish she'd forget him.'

This episode served as my first real-life exposure to adultery, its general theme and consequences. It was particularly memorable because, having had very limited experience of women and dating, I had a very romanticised vision of marriage. I looked forward to the day I would marry with happy excitement and often wondered who my wife would be. The loneliness I felt in Rabbinical seminary led me to believe that marriage incorporated everything that was good and loving, and could cure a person's desolation for ever. But here I was, before even having had my first date with a girl, and I had already become a cynic. There can be no human being with a feeling heart who could have witnessed this woman's grief, and her husband's pleading, or heard the words spoken by my friend without being adversely affected. This episode, coming as it did at the very end of my bachelorhood – thank God, I was engaged to my wife just three months later – served as the earliest inspiration for this book.

The ubiquitousness of infidelity

Adultery has become commonplace in modern society, especially among husbands. Though the statistics provided by different surveys, studies, and reports are not uniform, they all point to an overwhelming number of spouses who are finding sex outside marriage.

According to the latest survey carried out by the *Janus Report on Human Sexuality*, published in 1993, one in four middle-income men reported an *extraordinarily high* rate of regular and ongoing extramarital sex, while 8 per cent of women reported 'often and ongoing' extramarital sexual liaisons. Among women, a survey conducted by *Cosmopolitan* magazine in the mid-eighties came up with the startling fact that 51 per cent of its female readers had committed adultery. Similarly, in 1989, *New York Woman* magazine polled its readers and reported that almost one out of every two wives surveyed had cheated on their husbands.

The evidence leaves no doubt that adultery comes more commonly to men than to women, just as commitment comes more easily to women than to men. But perhaps the greatest indication of the phenomenal rise in adultery, and an even more shocking finding in the area of human sexual relations, is the admission, in the more recent studies of human sexual behaviour, of gross marital infidelity on the part of the very religious. Clearly, the very religious of various denominations are not necessarily practising what they preach. The *Janus Report* records that a third of all 'very religious' respondents, and 26 per cent of all 'religious' respondents, admitted having had extramarital affairs 'at least once', with 16 per cent of the 'very religious' admitting to 'often and ongoing' extramarital affairs. Furthermore, the authors remark, 'Another finding may be even more disturbing, given the faith many Americans have in religion as the strongest curtailer of illicit passion: the very religious were *most likely* to report often and ongoing adultery.' There is no doubt that these statistics are alarming. And yet, I have long been convinced that it is specifically within a religious framework that not just marriage, but passion in marriage, can best be maintained and developed. Those who disparage religion as being repressive are not correct. Judaism, for example, has never advocated sexual repression, but rather calls upon humans to focus all their sexual energy on their chosen partner.

Is monogamy viable?

A far more serious question that arises from all the above is at the heart of civilised Western living and the Judaeo-Christian ethic: is monogamy viable? Was it ever viable? In the face of such widespread marital infidelity, must we not really begin to question whether monogamy is not just some wishful fantasy born of religious mores?

From all indications it would appear that marriage is on the decline, while divorce and adultery are on the rise. These trends surely point to the failure of sexual monogamy as a way of life, and are certainly not very encouraging to young people contemplating marriage. Monogamy is simply not viable – according to statistics.

Is adultery positive?

Many people even argue that extramarital affairs are a good thing, healthy for marriage, and should not be decried at all. Innumerable psychologists, researchers and authors maintain that at times having a lover on the side can help to keep husbands and wives together. In study after study, many married men and women assert that, while they desire to remain married, the only thing that enables them to do so is the fact that they are having extramarital affairs. In many instances, a good marriage will be missing one component – sexual passion, for example – which can sometimes be provided only by someone outside the marriage. In other cases, what leads one partner into adultery is the desire to experiment and 'see what one is missing' in a monogamous relationship. If this adulterous affair satisfies such curiosity, and so leads to the long-term viability of the marriage, then what makes it so wrong?

In her *Report on Female Sexuality*, expert sex therapist Shere Hite quotes an unfaithful wife: 'I required love and sex – both together when possible. I could not have survived had I not fulfilled these needs, so [the affair] enriched my life and helped me to seek a good platonic relationship in my marriage, which actually saved the marriage. My husband did not know.' Whilst it is dubious in what sense the marriage could be said to have been 'saved', and whether 'a good platonic relationship' is what should be sought, this is a typical case of a married person looking outside the marriage for something he/she feels is lacking within it. Hite concludes, 'The condescension and lack of emotional closeness women are experiencing in their marriages is having a disastrous effect on women's ability to survive emotionally while staying completely within a marriage. Thus, for many women, having an outside relationship is one of the few ways to stay in the marriage. Having an affair can put new love and humanity into one's world, enabling one to go on living.'

Of course, these 'benefits' of an adulterous affair are counterbalanced by all the pain suffered by everyone concerned. Another of Hite's female respondents observed, 'Overall, though, I think the effects have been emotionally harmful, because there is no way to carry the relationship through to a happy ending. It must always end sadly. There is always hurt.' Indeed, adultery serves not to alleviate the problems in a marriage, but to run away from them. Surely it is better for a couple to rediscover love and passion in their relationship than to seek it with someone else, when it cannot last. Marriages are not saved when more complications are thrown in their way.

Yet, observing the meteoric rise in adultery statistics, I am amazed that one thing still has not changed: the almost universal condemnation which adultery receives. In this modern age where old scruples and religious teachings have largely been consigned to the dust heap of history, attitudes towards adultery have not. Although, as I have mentioned, there are those who would argue that adultery may have positive consequences, such opinions are not generally aired within mainstream society and they specifically call attention to themselves because of their rarity.

To quote from the *Independent on Sunday*'s front page, following a comprehensive survey in the wake of a recent scandal in which two leading Conservative ministers were revealed to have been having adulterous affairs, 'Whatever the failings of their political leaders, the British people are overwhelmingly in favour of monogamy. Nearly 80 per cent consider extramarital sex to be always or mostly wrong, thus echoing Dr George Carey, the Archbishop of Canterbury, who denounced adultery as a sin yesterday. But the large majority of people see nothing wrong in premarital sex.'

Adultery – one of the last taboos

Since the beginning of the 20th century, attitudes have changed so much that openness about and public ack-nowledgement of everything from premarital sex, homosexuality and group sex, to male prostitution and explicitly erotic literature and films, are now wide-spread. So why is it that, when virtually every form of human sexual behaviour is now accepted or even encouraged, adultery alone is still thoroughly and universally condemned?

Premarital sex is not only no longer condemned, but those who abstain are seen as old-fashioned, indeed as a bit barmy. According to the *Janus Report*, over 80 per cent of men obtain extensive sexual experience before marriage, and I suspect, having served as Rabbi to university students for six years, that the numbers are far higher. Before the turn of the century this would have been unthinkable, but premarital sex has now definitely become the norm.

The same can be said of many other so-called 'sexual vices'. Just a few decades ago homosexuality was not only condemned, but actually prohibited by American civil law in over 24 states. Yet today mainstream society would label as a demagogue and fascist anyone who condemned homosexuals in public. Homosexuality has come a long way from being labelled 'a crime against Nature' as recently as a century ago, and a 'human medical pathology' up to only 30 years ago, to being accepted as a viable 'alternative lifestyle' in the modern age.

This also applies to group sex. While it may not be as widespread as premarital sex, the *Janus Report* claims that 17 per cent of men found group sex 'very normal' or 'all right'. A far greater number actually admitted to having been involved in group sex. In fact, there are very few sexual deviances left which society refuses to tolerate or which have not been labelled 'normal' and routine. In *Janus*'s words, 'Much of what [Freud] considered deviant has become part of the everyday sex lives of many Americans.' Similarly, 'Many sexual practices that were once deemed wrong or sick or forbidden appear to be commonplace today.'

I can see only two exceptions to this rule. The first is child sex and abuse, which is still seen as evil and hideous; the other is adultery. Society still views those who molest children as being sick and in need of serious psychological help, not to mention deserving of severe retribution and punishment.

But what can we make of the lingering distaste, indeed revulsion, toward adulterers? Whereas child abusers prey on helpless innocents, and their crime goes against the grain of everything we hold dear in this world, the same does not apply to an adulterous husband or wife. There must be a reason for our loathing and deep disrespect for those who cheat on their spouses, and why we warm to the message of films like *Fatal Attraction* and *Indecent Proposal*. Both of these portray the terrible damage that adultery brings in its wake, and we witness the pain and desperation wrought by an act of infidelity.

Commenting after the aforementioned governmental controversy, the Archbishop of Canterbury added, 'Adultery and the breakdown of faithfulness and trust that it represents is more than a mere indiscretion. It's a sin. It is a failure to live up to the kind of standards we expect from all people in authority . . . It cannot be said that reliable evidence of hypocrisy, untrustworthiness, irresponsibility or selfishness in one aspect of life is irrelevant to a person's general credibility. People do not switch morality on and off like a light bulb.'

I disagree. The nature of human sexuality is such that it is impulsive and instinctive and therefore does indeed switch on and off like a light bulb. We all know that there are moments when we feel intensely sexual, and other moments when the entire sexual enterprise seems uninteresting and even rather odd. On the whole, however, men and woman gravitate toward each other naturally. It is precisely for this reason that Judaism forbade unmarried men and women to allow themselves to be alone together in secluded settings which may lead to compromising situations. Judaism recognizes that men and women are first and foremost *sexual* beings, and this recognition is a compliment to both. The fact that some people may fall prey to human nature does not automatically disqualify them from public office, or even seriously compromise their integrity. Committing adultery, however heinous we believe the act to be, is not a total statement of what a man or woman is or of his or her morality.

To state that someone who commits adultery will definitely be untrustworthy in his public life is to assume that both are indiscriminate forms of dishonesty. They are not. When we discover that a man or a woman has committed adultery, the question that should really be asked is not why they have done so, but rather, *why didn't it take place sooner?* Why did they agree to monogamy in the first place? As we shall see, it is marriage and monogamy that are totally unnatural, while adultery and polygamy are in complete consonance with the natural state of man. One does not *choose* to commit adultery. Rather, one is naturally pulled in that direction, and must choose *not* to commit adultery. Adultery is prevented when a man or a woman makes a conscious decision to apply the brakes. Other forms of untrustworthiness, such as theft, involve a conscious effort to *commit* the crime, rather than to prevent oneself from the transgression.

There is perhaps no clearer case in point than the example of the great humanitarian hero Oskar Schindler. He was a wretched husband, who cheated on his wife on numerous occasions and finally even left her. And yet he risked all to save 1000 helpless Jews. And ever since the publication of Thomas Keneally's best-selling *Schindler's Ark*, and the screening of Steven Spielberg's epic *Schindler's List*, countless writers have asked, how could so awful a husband have been so great a humanitarian? But what is the meaning of the question? There is simply no significant relation between the two. The fact that you cheat in your marriage does not reflect an overall character defect. It does mean that you are not making a strong enough effort to channel all your sexual passion into your marriage, and the result is a terrible sin which leads to your spouse's fathomless pain, and must, of course, be corrected.

Adultery within a marriage

Although about one in five divorcees of either gender cite extramarital affairs as the primary cause of their divorce, some extramarital sexual activity can apparently occur within an otherwise stable marriage

25

without causing a breakdown. The *Janus Report* found that 28 per cent of married men and women had had more than one extramarital sexual contact without their marriages dissolving.

Nevertheless, it is patently obvious that extramarital affairs are poor ingredients for a trusting marriage. In the time that I have counselled married couples I have found there are understandably numerous examples of marriages dissolving, often violently, after one single case of infidelity.

But I have also been involved in many cases where the wife or husband is highly forgiving of the other's infidelity, and believes that their love for each other is far more important than a momentary breach of their marital bond. More often than not this happens in cases where the spouse is honest enough to inform their partner of their unfaithfulness. The very first casualty of adultery in any marriage is the trust upon which the marriage is built, and this is somewhat reinstated by the spouse's unprompted confession. But if the marriage is healthy enough to sustain the impact of an affair on either side, why did this not prevent it from happening in the first place?

I believe wholeheartedly that adulterous acts and adulterous behaviour do not necessarily betray any serious problems within a marriage. In fact, adultery is far more a statement about human nature than it is about the state of matrimony. I say this with one important proviso, however: it applies only to acts of adultery committed by the husband. While acts of adultery on the part of either spouse are equally sinful and equally serious, it is the wife's straying that is indicative of a serious problem within the marriage.

When a husband is unfaithful, often the cause is not his marriage at all, but a natural sexual predisposition towards variety. When a wife commits adultery it is not because of her nature but rather because of her *marriage*. Husbands frequently state that even if they stray they still love their wives and they are doing nothing really to hurt the marriage. Many of them actually believe, however mistakenly, that their acts of infidelity do not seriously affect their married lives. Later in this book I will demonstrate the fallacy of their thinking.

There is a well-documented difference between men's reasons and women's reasons for committing adultery. The large number of men who admit that they do so although they are very much in love with their wives seems to tell us that men do not look for strong emotional attachments with their girlfriends and mistresses. *In the minds of many adulterous men, love is something they get from their wives; excitement is something they get from their mistresses.* They often talk themselves into the belief that they are unhappily married and their wives don't understand them, when really all they are feeling is boredom brought about by a natural inclination away from monogamy. Emotional fulfilment has little or nothing to do with it.

Many commentators maintain that a husband's or wife's adultary is an indication that something is seriously, even irrevocably, wrong with their marriage. In contrast, I believe not only that in most cases a marriage should not break up as a result of a sexual indiscretion, but moreover, as I shall argue throughout this book, that it is specifically the *possibility* of adultery that can resolve the greatest of all challenges to marriage: the loss of sexual passion in long-term relationships.

Adultery is a sin of omission

What is the true sin of adultery? It is a sin of omission. People seem to think adultery is a sin of *commission*: you do wrong, therefore it is a transgression. But it is not. It is a void. It is wrong not because you have done something wrong, but because *you haven't done something right*. All of the affection, emotion, and attention you lavish on the person you seek to seduce should be shown to your spouse. Instead of putting it into your marriage you're focusing outside your marriage. A marriage is a hungry animal, an electric, alive institution. It needs to be constantly fed with attention, devotion and love.

In my first year at Oxford a 25-year-old woman wanted to be divorced after only two years of marriage. Why? Because her husband had been unfaithful to her. She caught him red-handed in the matrimonial bed with another woman. She was hysterical. 'Out!' she cried to the woman who was scrambling to find her clothes. After she had left, she shouted and cried to her husband at the top of her lungs, 'You're a beast, you're an animal. You brought that whore into my house and into our bed. How could you?' And she cried and cried for three weeks, inconsolable, until she just decided that she was leaving him. I was on very good terms with both of them, and struggled to try and keep their marriage together. I said to her, 'Look, Judaism is a forgiving religion and people deserve a second chance, so if he feels regret then why won't you forgive him?'

'Shmuley,' she said to me, 'I don't want the divorce only because he committed this abomination. Had he been a husband the rest of the time – had he been considerate, compassionate, caring, loving; had he called me when he was away, been concerned when I was unwell, or complimented me on the efforts I made to enrich and beautify myself for him – then I might be able to overlook it. But he has never acted like a husband. He never helped with the housework, and never even took the time to talk to me and tell me what was happening in his life. If he is not a husband at all, then why should I overlook his mistake? I can forgive my *husband* for doing something wrong, but this man is a stranger. Love can assuage hurt. But here there is no love.' I use this story to illustrate a very important principle: adultery is not about hurting your wife. Rather, it is about taking the affection and desire that are hers by marital right and giving them away to a stranger. *By committing adultery you do not become an adulterer. Rather, you cease being a spouse.*

From time immemorial it has been debated whether or not a man or a woman can love two people at once. Can a husband love his wife and his mistress equally? Can a woman remain focused on her husband and her paramour simultaneously? But the question is immaterial. Even if a man could *love* his wife and his mistress simultaneously, he still could not show them both enough attention and affection to sustain his relationship properly with either of them. The same applies even more so to women, who seem to get more emotionally involved in their extramarital affairs. And marriages do not thrive on what we *feel*. Rather, they live through *what we do* about our feelings. That is what is most important in every marriage. No wonder, then, that the way in which husbands and wives most often find out about each other's affairs is not directly, but *indirectly*. It is not through walking in on one's husband while he is with his girlfriend, or hearing about it from a friend. Rather, the process is far more subtle, and usually begins with noticing that one's spouse is distracted. No longer are they as loving, attentive, or concerned. Their thoughts are far away and their sexual desire for their spouse is usually very much diminished.

Psychologist Carol Botwin describes in her book *Tempted Women* the change in an adulterous wife's behaviour that so often betrays her: 'You stop trying to change things that were bothering you before. If you felt that you weren't getting enough sex, you stop attempting to entice your husband. If you were complaining that he didn't communicate enough, you stop trying to open him up. If he drank too much or had other bad habits, you stop railing at him about them. After finding some satisfaction and fulfilment with the other man, you give up on your husband and stop bothering him about things that you were carrying on about before.'

Thus, adultery serves as a double wrong, first because it betrays a marriage and causes terrible pain to one's spouse, and second because it robs a marriage of the input it needs to survive and prosper. On a more individual level adultery erodes, if not utterly destroys, the faith and trust that one partner has in the other. Worse, it causes an almost incurable feeling of inadequacy that the partner who has been cheated on cannot shake. 'What do I lack that he found with someone else?' the wife asks herself. 'Have I not been loving or caring enough?' the husband asks himself. What is particularly unjust about this introspection is that it is the *victim* who feels responsible.

This feeling of inadequacy is particularly acute when the betrayed spouse feels that the areas in which he or she is seen to be deficient just cannot be changed. It is one thing for a spouse to feel that perhaps because they focused too intently on their career, they showed too little affection to their partner; this can be re-dressed. But what if the wife discovers that her husband's lover is unusually beautiful and sexy, or the husband finds out that his wife's lover is far more successful than he is, or better-looking and of more athletic build? How can either of them avoid the feeling of being an inferior lover, and being unable to compete?

Causes of adultery

I much enjoyed Naura Hayden's book *How to Satisfy a Woman Every Time*. Although it has quite a risqué title, the book is actually about bringing passion into *marriage*, and I commend the author for her beautiful statements about marriage. 'Now we come to my favourite subject, marriage . . . I truly believe in the commitment of marriage. I think it's the greatest rela-tionship that two people can ever have. A partnership with someone who loves you. What could be better. I hate it when a married man makes a play for me. Even if he's the handsomest, most darling man-about-town, it truly distresses me. I don't want him to embarrass his wife by flirting outrageously with me or any other woman.' But even she falls prey to the belief that adultery is usually a statement about the problems within a marriage: 'I believe most of it stems from incomplete sex lives. The men fooling around are doing it because they sense their wives are not deeply in love with them. Most women are deeply dissatisfied sexually with their husbands and their marriages, and are looking around for "Mr Right" to fulfil them in this very important way.'

Nonsense! Many men who fool around are fully aware that their wives are completely in love with them; in fact, this is often the very reason for adultery. When a wife loves her husband too much and shows too much devotion, and never any sign of being sexually attracted to another man, and conversely no men show an interest in her, the husband searches elsewhere for excitement: his wife presents no challenge to him, and no flattery since, on the surface, no one else seems interested in her. Men want a woman who is desirable to others as well. The greatest cause of adultery among men is not a search for 'deep emotional love', but *a failing to see one's wife as a desirable woman*. It can hardly be erotic and sexually seductive to see one's spouse first and foremost not as a woman but as 'my wife'. As soon as a man discovers that his wife is sexually interested in another man, and that others are interested in her, he goes crazy and wants her back. The reason: he now recognises that indeed she is not merely *his wife*, but an attractive sexual creature, and that itself makes her irresistibly desirable.

So, while a bad sex life may not be the *cause* of adultery, it almost certainly will be the *result*. Since men are not naturally monogamous, if they do not make an effort to transcend their natures and focus all their sexual energy on their wives, their wives will feel deeply dissatisfied with their intimate lives, because their husbands are simply not wholeheartedly participating in it. They may then embark on a quest for 'Mr Right', and even if they do not, they will be deeply discontented with their husbands. This in turn will cause husbands to feel that they are not fully loved, which, at least in the short term, is true. Love, as King Solomon so beautifully reflected in 'Song of Songs', is largely reciprocal – 'like the waters of the sea that reflect the human face, so too the heart reciprocates the emotions shown to it'. Of course, this spiral of dissatisfaction just continues to corrode the relationship, unless a stop is put to it.

The idea that any man or woman who is not married to a sexual tigress or tiger, or who has not read every sex manual and experimented with every sexual position, will of necessity feel unfulfilled, is erroneous. It is not *positions* that men and women want in sex, but *attention*. There is nothing so erotic as the knowledge that the partner you are with is totally interested in you, and only you. They delight in just looking at your body, and gauging your response to the activities they initiate. The ultimate turn-off is to feel that your partner is not fully interested in you, or that their thoughts are elsewhere. Even the sexiest prostitute, with all the sexual knowledge in the world, is not worth a penny for her favours. There can never exist any deep erotic pleasure with her since *she is being paid*. Come to your senses! She is just not interested. She couldn't give a damn about you, and every erotic movement and sound she makes is contrived.

I once heard a sex therapist speaking on CNN. Interestingly, she was herself a former prostitute. She said that whenever she counsels couples about marriage, she walks over to the husband and asks him to point to his principal sexual organ. Inevitably, the man blushes, and instinctively looks down to the area of his crotch. She then says, 'Wrong! This is your most powerful sexual organ,' pointing to his head. 'It is the interest you have in a person that turns them on.' This is absolutely true. Sexual excitement and elation lie in the mind, not in the genitals.

It is for this reason that marriage, and marriage only, possesses the greatest erotic potential. Since marriage involves the greatest commitment, it is also the greatest statement of interest. It is a statement by two people that they are so interested in each other that they are even prepared to close off all other sexual possibilities and partners. To make the marital bond effective it is necessary to see it primarily as a sexual commitment. Instead of seeing a marriage proposal only as a statement of 'He loves me and therefore he wants to spend the rest of his life with me,' we must equally view it in these terms: 'He sees me as so sexually desirable that he wishes to spend all his days talking with me, *and also his nights with me in my bed.*'

But, conversely, this can also serve as the reason why *adultery* can be so exciting. A woman who has an affair with a married man might be prepared to put all her ethical scruples, and the knowledge of the hurt that she is causing another woman, on the back-burner, since she says to herself, 'Can you imagine how attracted this guy is to me? He is prepared to sacrifice everything for me. He is risking *everything* for me. He really loves me.' Regardless of how terrible the consequences of the adulterous act may be, the man still wants her, and cannot deny her attraction. And for many women, the man's passionate interest in them serves as an offer so inviting they just can't turn it down. What we all want, above all else, is to be adored and needed.

But this too is a farce. He is not prepared to sacrifice everything for you, even if he says he is. In fact, he sacrifices nothing. It is all an illusion. He uses you secretly and in the process loses nothing but his own innocence. He keeps his wife, and children, and has commitment-free sex with you. In his mind, there is no risk, since he is sure he will not be caught. And even if he is, he thinks his wife will forgive him, rather than risk divorce and the breakdown of the family, and life will go on as before. If he truly does love you, then why does he not carry on his affair with you in public? Let him celebrate and proclaim his association with you to the whole world, including his wife.

The marriage commitment

Marriage does not come easy to anyone who undertakes its commitments. Nor should it. I have always believed that the greatest statement of love from one human being to another is when a constant, ongoing effort is made to remain loyal, faithful, loving and caring amidst the natural inclination to selfishness, apathy, and sexual experimentation. Any husband and wife for whom marriage comes easy are deprived of making that most sublime statement to each other, that is, I love you so much that I seek to transcend my nature by remaining totally focused on you at all times.

Anything in life whose attainment does not require great effort is simply not worth having. Marriage is the greatest demonstration of this. There is nothing more special, more loving, more worthwhile, more sublime, and better able to cure humankind's hurts and woes than marriage, when it is done right. But, equally, there is nothing so miserable, hurtful, devastating or tormenting to the soul as marriage when it goes wrong. We must therefore make an effort, our greatest effort, to be at all times loving, caring, and faithful partners, even while we feel a natural attraction to men and women outside our marriage. Monogamy is not a concession that religion asks humans to make in the name of holiness and decency. On the contrary, it is the very vehicle through which the ultimate sexual passion can be experienced and sustained to make our marriages pleasurable, glorious, and above all holy.

2

The unnatural state of marriage

The potential and natural inclination towards adultery is especially highlighted by the extreme unnaturalness of marriage. Every human being is first and foremost non-monogamous, and only after an effort is made and sexual focus attained do we become monogamous.

A woman came to see me in Oxford. She was already hysterical when she walked in, and I wondered how I could calm her down. Susan, a young wife of 33, had been referred to me by a colleague in London after discovering that her husband had had a six-week affair with a woman he had met on an aeroplane. When Susan found out, her husband did his utmost to dissuade her from leaving him. They had three children and he had called me and begged me to help keep the marriage together. But whatever arguments I used to persuade her to forgive him, she wouldn't listen. She just kept ranting and raving, 'How could he? I gave him the best years of his life. How *could* he?' Finally, I bent over my desk, looking her in the eyes, and said, 'How could he *not*?' She looked startled and hurt, and turned to leave. Before she did so, I explained myself.

So many people make the mistake of asking how a spouse can stray. On the contrary, the real question is how could they remain faithful! Make no mistake about it, adultery is what is natural and intuitive. It is marriage and monogamy that run against the grain of human nature. So the real question is not 'How can anyone commit adultery?' but, 'How can anyone commit themselves to marriage and monogamy in the first place, and what can we do to make people behave *unnaturally* and remain faithful?' I told Susan that what was surprising about her husband's behaviour was not that he had committed adultery, but rather that he was ever faithful in the first place. I advised her that an understanding of the inherently promiscuous nature of all humans might perhaps lead her to be more forgiving, so long as her husband firmly undertook never again to repeat this terrible mistake, and acted towards her more affectionately.

Let's take a closer look at this. Is it natural to be married? Is it an automatic human impulse? Is marriage an intuitive culmination of desire on the part of single beings to join together and thereby permanently assuage their loneliness? And, most importantly, is monogamy natural?

The answer is an emphatic NO! Forget it. Monogamy is as unnatural as the desire to remain hungry. I contend without any reservation whatsoever that marriage is not a natural human state. I further contend that the knowledge that marriage is not natural is the single most important element in any successful marriage, and the more quickly we realise it, the better, because we will then be on guard constantly to make our marriages work. Judaism maintains that the fundamental challenge of human living is for man to rise above his nature. We dare not allow our natures to rule us. Rather, we must endeavour to exert our mastery over our own human inclination. Only then can we be guaranteed fulfilling and extraordinary lives which are not the product of mere impulse.

I read a story once about a white Bengal tiger in the Miami Zoo who ate a zoo keeper. It was decided not to destroy the animal. Part of the reason was that the white Bengal tiger is virtually extinct already. But the more important consideration was that the zoo keeper himself had made the fatal mistake of leaving the cage open as he fed the animal. It was felt that the animal should not be punished merely because of its predatory and voracious nature in the face of human error. But such clemency would never be granted a human. He would be expected to rise above his nature. If you are sitting innocently in a bar, and a man comes up and repeatedly insults you and provokes you, you'll end up going to jail and possibly even the electric chair if you take out a gun and shoot him. Because you're human, you are expected to control your emotions, and will be held accountable for your actions.

The same applies to humankind's natural gravitation to many sexual partners. The fact that your nature leads you to stray will never serve as an adequate excuse for hurting your spouse and destroying your marriage. Therefore, when we speak of 'holy matrimony', and when we speak of marriage as a godly institution, we should attune our ears to the serious implications of these words, namely, that *marriage is not a natural institution*, but a supernatural one. We do not slide comfortably into marriage or monogamy; they must be worked upon, and we must never take them for granted.

Imagine if I made you the offer of a lifetime: a beautiful country mansion is yours, with every luxury and amenity provided, at 50 per cent below market price. I will sell it to you, but with one caveat: you must move into the house and never move out again. You cannot sell it or rent it out. It's wonderful, but you are absolutely stuck with it. There may be some slight provisions for moving out, but they will be accompanied by severe financial penalties, emotional drainage and pain. Are you still interested? Or do you see the catch?

What if I offer you a great bargain on a car, but along the same lines: will you purchase it? And if you do, are you sure that when a younger, more modern and better-equipped model is released, you won't regret your earlier life-long commitment? While your car ages and loses its original gloss and shine, will you not look with envy at your neighbour's more up-to-date purchase?

Those of you who aren't taken by either of these offers, now ask yourself, *why then are you prepared to be married?* In fact, there is no other circumstance in life where an individual is prepared to commit themselves, amidst any possible eventuality, to a life-long prospect. How could we? How would we know that things wouldn't go wrong? I am not so naive as to deny the power of love. But if you are indeed so infatuated with someone that you wish to marry them, go ahead and live with them! Hold them in your arms and make them yours. But for God's sake, don't be silly enough to say things like 'Till death us do part,' or 'I will love you for ever,' when you have no guarantee that you will wish to preserve the relationship 50 years hence. Take things gradually, see how it goes. It's the reasonable, logical thing to do. You wouldn't commit yourself this way to anything else. Why, then, to marriage?

Had God never thought up marriage, human beings wouldn't have either

The answer is that marriage is not a human, but a *divine* institution. It is irrational; it really doesn't make sense. I suggest sincerely that if God had not commanded us to enter into marriage, mankind would never have come up with it. To be sure, we might have devised some vaguely committed style of living together, but it would be entirely predicated on the emotions of the moment, and with no provision for commitment into what is at best a questionable future. We are all only too aware of the unpredictability of emotions. The partner you can't live without today, you can't live with tomorrow. Men and women might have made a life together and be waiting around to see how long it lasts; how long the sexual and emotional attachment retains its passion and magic. But why the commitment under the wedding canopy?

It is specifically religious communities that have the highest rate of marriage and at the youngest age. Elsewhere, the average couple are finding increasingly little reason to marry and are opting to live together instead, often with no intention to marry whatsoever. Why on earth should they? They love each other and in their minds this is sufficient. Without religion, marriage would surely never have been invented.

If marriage were a logical and/or moral imperative, if it were a human creation, it would be gaining strength in this age of rationalism. But the historical fact remains that many great rationalists, indeed many great philosophers, have always been fiercely opposed to marriage, viewing it as the most oppressive of all institutions. The *Oxford Dictionary of Quotations* lists 62 entries on the subject of marriage. Only four are positive, a few neutral, and the rest, over 50, very negative. The consensus is that getting married is about as satisfying as root canal, rather than a route to happiness.

I especially like this supremely cynical quote from George Bernard Shaw's *Man and Superman*: 'Those who talk most about the blessings of marriage and the constancy of its vows are the very people who declare that if the chain were broken and the prisoners left free to choose, the whole social fabric would fly asunder. You cannot have the argument both ways. If the prisoner is happy, why lock him in? If he is not, why pretend that he is?'

Shaw must have known that his assumption that those who are married are not happy would strike a chord with a great many of his readers. No, marriage is not natural, and the belief that it is has led to terrible misconceptions and inestimable damage in relationships. Happiness in marriage, unlike the passion of adultery, requires effort. And because it is a divine rather than human construct it requires the blessing of Heaven to endure. Every endeavour to bring greater depth into married life through spiritual and religious observances and closeness can only strengthen the marital bond.

'The person I married is not the one I fell in love with'

A common contemporary complaint among married couples is that things change once they get married. They often feel that the person whom they married is different, sometimes radically, from the person they were dating, who was somehow more sensitive, more caring, and more responsive. In the words of a female friend, 'The probability that my husband would open the car door for me now, as he did when we were dating, is the same probability that I would bring him breakfast in bed, as I did every Sunday in our first few months of marriage.'

When the couple first started going out, he was on his best behaviour, always careful to be a gentleman. Now, here they are married just four months and already he belches in his wife's presence and digs out the wax in his ears, not even noticing how disgusted his wife is with this vulgarity.

How can this be? Whence spring these changes? Does marriage have a magical, yet sinister capacity for transforming a woman from Snow White into Lady Macbeth or a man from Doctor Jekyll into Mr Hyde? Why is it that so often marriage is not nearly as pleasant or exciting as dating? It is this reality that has given rise to the oft-repeated aphorism, 'How to kill a great relationship? Get married.'

The real explanation lies in couples' mistaken belief that it is natural to be married. Whereas when they date they exert every effort to impress their intended partner, when they finally marry they suddenly exert no effort at all, thinking that bliss will just flow automatically from their union. They do not see marriage as a constant struggle, a constant challenge, in which a person must be on alert at all times. Rather, once you get married, you need hardly do anything at all. You simply stay married. In her book *The Erotic Silence of the American Wife*, sociologist Dalma Heyn identifies the problem in the context of a theory that some men

are what sociologists call 'situationally expressive' –
loving and forthcoming during courtship, when they
are eager to win a woman, but inclined to withdraw
expressiveness once they win her.

Everyone knows that in order to build up and sustain
attraction with a member of the opposite sex, one must
work very hard. To be sure, there often is love at first
sight, or an immediate attraction. You meet in a restaurant, and you just know that you would love to go out
with the girl sitting at table number seven. But even
this sort of attraction will dissipate almost immediately
if nothing is done about it. If you do not ask her out,
you will forget about her quite rapidly. If you do ask
her out, you must do your utmost to impress her. Why
else should she be interested?

When a man and a woman date, they are always on
their best behaviour, displaying the most attractive
aspects of their personalities in order to create a
favourable impression. I remember this well from my
own experience. I was a student in New York with
no means of transportation when I first took out the
woman I wanted to marry and whom I was eager to
impress. We went out to dinner to a beautiful kosher
Chinese restaurant in Manhattan. A cab-driver offered
us a ride back to Brooklyn, and on the way back I asked
him if he knew of a car rental company who would
rent a car in New York to someone under the age of 25.

He drove us to Coney Island Avenue in Brooklyn,
saying he had a friend he could speak to who required
a $300 deposit since I was under 25, in addition to the
$200 fee for a week's rental. He told me to give him the
money so he could negotiate with his friend, and gave
me his car keys as 'security'. The three of us got out of

the cab and walked towards an office that said 'Car Rental'. Suddenly, like a bolt of lightning he ran back into the cab, obviously possessed of a spare set of keys, and was gone, into the wild blue yonder, together with my $500.

I was a poor student and the blow was devastating. I will say as an extreme understatement that I was angry. My first instinct was to erupt and verbally consign him and his offspring for a thousand generations to the nether reaches of hell, a place where I had consigned many such scoundrels before. But I looked to my right and there was this woman who was innocent enough to have been genuinely puzzled and troubled by what had just happened. 'Is he coming back?' she asked. 'No,' I said. 'I've been ripped off.' She clearly wondered what my response would be.

I sighed, and then said in a quiet voice, 'Poor devil. Can you just imagine how impoverished he must be, how desperately he needs the money, to have had to resort to that act of connivance and theft? I wish him well with the money, and may God look after him. After all, we are all human and have our faults. And just as I would not like others to judge me, so I too overlook the infraction of this poor lost soul.' There was not a shred of sincerity in those words and never in my life have I uttered something so disingenuously. In fact, I wanted to tar and feather the man, and then stuff him into the engine of a 747 jumbo jet. But it worked. And Debbie, who was later to marry me (poor soul), gave me a deep and satisfying look and said, 'I can't believe it. The average guy would have been so angry, would have wished him dead. But you – you're so kind and loving. You're amazing.'

So much for knowing your partner before marriage . . .

We all recognise the need to show our most caring side in wooing a member of the opposite sex with a view to marriage. We know that it just doesn't happen *naturally*. People don't fall for each other if they don't *do* anything for each other. People will not commit themselves to a life-long endeavour impetuously.

But then, finally, after a laborious and time-consuming courtship, he gets on his knee and pops the big question – and it's worked. She blushes and with elation says yes. The big day comes, and now they are married. What now? He is no longer on his best behaviour, but loses his temper frequently and with little cause. Nor is he as generous, complaining that they must save all their money to pay the mortgage. Nor is she as patient with him, or as loving as she once was. They sit around with their heads in their hands wondering what went wrong.

And yet the answer is staring them in the face. They have made the mistake of assuming that once a couple get married, the process of impressing each other is over. But marriage is not just a single act; it is a constant process, and we must always engage ourselves not just in *being* married, but in *becoming* married. Marriage is not a natural state, and our natural resistance to its monogamous demands and huge commitment necessitates a constant and conscious effort to make it successful.

Marriage needs constant nourishment

The knowledge that we never *become* married, but rather must always *engage in the process of becoming married*, can have enormous implications for passion in marriage. I mention elsewhere that the words *lover* or *mistress* carry with them an erotic mystique. So do the words *man* and *woman*. But the words *husband* and *wife* do not. To think of your wife not as a *woman* but as a *wife* is to consign her to the realm of familiarity and boredom. The knowledge that none of us ever becomes a wife or a husband, but always remains just a man or a woman trying to remain faithful despite a powerful inclination to do otherwise, serves as a constant reminder that we are married to sexual creatures who are not naturally monogamous and who are deeply attractive to others. We must therefore work to preserve their loyalty always by showing them love, attention, and romance. Remember this all-important rule: no one ever *becomes* married, and no man or woman ever becomes a husband or wife. Rather, they, just like you, are alive and alert sexual beings who must ward off their attraction to strangers constantly and reaffirm their sexual fidelity to you specifically and realign their sexual energy accordingly. This knowledge is the first major step in reinvigorating a stale and boring marriage. Do not take your spouse's fidelity for granted.

That no man or woman ever becomes a husband or wife is reflected in the Bible. There is no word for 'wife', for example, in Biblical Hebrew. Rather the word is *eishes*, which translates as 'the woman of'. Thus, Sarah was 'the woman of Abraham', rather than his wife.

The only success we will ever have in marriage is if

we always focus on what we can put into marriage, not just on what we can take out of it. As a Rabbi, I hear all too often young couples complaining that they do not 'get anything' from the relationship. Before marriage a man and woman are separate and distinct beings. If they are to join together as one, they both must reach inward towards each other, constantly contributing to each other. But if they focus on what they receive from each other, instead of what they can give, then both are reaching outward, effectively *away* from each other. How then can they be joined? This is especially so with regard to human sexuality. If indeed monogamy is unnatural, then we must do all we can to make our intimate lives passionate and exciting enough to satisfy our spouse.

This should not sound radical because I am not arguing that we do not deserve any benefits from marriage. Nor am I suggesting that there are no legitimate needs on the part of each spouse in a marriage. If both husband and wife focus on what they can *contribute* to a marriage, both will be receiving and enjoying the benefits of companionship and marriage not as strangers, but as loving halves of an indivisible whole.

3

Do men and women *need* many sexual partners?

'Women are more naturally monogamous than men. It is a biological necessity. When promiscuity prevails, they will always be more often the victims than the culprits. Also domestic happiness is more necessary to them than to us, and the quality by which they most easily hold a man, their beauty, decreases every year after they come to maturity.'

C. S. Lewis, 'We have no right to happiness'
Saturday Evening Post, 1963

What do you make of the following wife's complaint: 'My husband has not been faithful to me. How do I feel? Mad with fury. I am angry and it hurts. It is like having some kind of illness that is slowly eating away at me. I cannot just turn off my feelings and simply stop loving him like I was turning off a light. I want my husband to be monogamous. I don't think I am expecting or asking for anything more than he is asking and expecting of me. The worst thing he has ever done is sleep in another woman's bed when he should have been at home with me in our bed.'

Is the statement reasonable? Is the woman correct in assuming that by expecting her husband to be faithful she is merely asking what he asks of her?

That monogamy is not a natural state for a man is a truth whether we approach it, like myself as a Rabbi, from the religious perspective, or even from a secular Western perspective. The theory of evolution maintains that man is a product of gradual development from the animal to the intellectual: not only is there a kinship between man and animals, but man *is* an animal, although endowed with higher cognitive faculties. Monogamy among male animals is extremely rare. It is one of the fundamental assumptions of evolution, through its essential mechanism of natural selection and the survival of the fittest, that the survival of a species depends on the males copulating and inseminating as many females as possible. Socio-biologists have long argued that the male is inherently promiscuous, going from partner to partner to ensure the most widespread possible distribution of his gene pool. This conclusion is supported indirectly by many sex researchers who cite numerous surveys showing that men are far more likely than women to have extramarital affairs.

Male sexuality

Whereas modern society is largely of the opinion that men and women differ chiefly, if not solely, with regard to their reproductive systems, the Bible maintains that men and women differ in many important respects (which of course have no bearing on their equality), but none so much as the area of human sexuality. It is in accordance with these differences that Judaism enacts different religious obligations, corresponding to the unique masculine and feminine traits possessed by each gender. Significantly, whereas the Bible does not countenance polyandry for women, and even considers it abomination, it does allow polygamy in theory for n although polygamy was not encouraged (partly of the enmity it creates between women, and se of the opposition from the majority – Christian population), the fact that the for men and not for women seems recognition of the natural differ- sexes. Abraham had two wives, ing David six, and Solomon topped at we understand to be hundreds. y was a concession made by the Bible to accommodate the natural male drive to seek more than one sexual partner. The Bible does, however, make the case that monogamy is a far better, holier state in which to live, and to which man should aspire (and later the Rabbis forbade polygamy as a Jewish lifestyle outright).

But the most impressive proof of this difference between men and women is, of course, empirical. It is *the women* themselves who are astounded at the natural male tendency to promiscuity, finding nothing within themselves, amidst a very strong sex drive, that would match men's inability to be satiated with one sexual partner. The *Hite Report* quotes many women who are flabbergasted at the unfaithfulness of some of their friends' husbands: 'I do not get involved with or date, nor have I ever even been attracted sexually to, a friend's husband, boyfriend, or date. But I sure have had my friends' husbands, boyfriends, dates, and friends try and do it with me – in fact, most of them. Usually when the guy makes a pass, I think, "What more does he want?" It seems many men are seeking newness, which they equate with passion. Newness meaning lots of women.'

Female sexuality

Many would refute the above conclusions by pointing out that studies reveal that women have nearly as many extramarital affairs as men, especially since the sexual revolution of the 1960s. In 1953, Alfred Kinsey found that 26 per cent of women were having sex outside their marriages. The *Hite Report*, published in 1987, indicated that 70 per cent of women married five years or more were having sex outside their marriages. Many other surveys have reached a similar conclusion that female infidelity, while not quite as high as men's, still reaches above 50 per cent – and is increasing.

But these figures can be misleading. The first important point to bear in mind is that, whereas male extramarital sex tends to be of the 'one-night stand' nature, that is, rapid and often, female infidelity tends to be far more of the long-lasting, emotionally involved type. What women covet far more than a sexual liaison is a loving partner; for them the sex is ancillary in an affair, whereas for men it is *central*.

In fact, among women, extramarital affairs rarely lead to divorce (only 17 per cent), but tend to continue in intense relationships as a stable way of life for years. The average length of wives' affairs that are not one- or two-time meetings, is, surprisingly, four years – longer than many marriages last these days. It seems curious that most women opt to stay in a marriage even when the love in the affair is deeper – although financial necessity and the unavailability of the man in question (since most married women's lovers are married themselves) would help account for this. We must conclude that women who divorce their husbands usually do so because of what is lacking in their marriage, not because they are in love with someone else.

'The majority of women having affairs say they feel alienated, emotionally closed out, or harassed in their marriages; for 60 per cent, having an affair is a way of enjoying oneself, reasserting one's identity, having one person appreciate you in a way that another doesn't,' writes Shere Hite. The adulterous women she goes on to quote were clearly seeking not just sex, but love and attention:

'I felt so unappreciated at home and was given "love" and appreciation in the relationship. The effect on me personally was to build me up, support me, and help me to cope with my marriage.'

'The reason for my affair for three years now has been hunger for affection. I told my husband several times I could not live without affection.'

'My husband chose to ignore me for years . . . and years . . . Eventually I started having affairs . . .'

Hite writes of the female nature: 'Women are not looking for affairs basically for "more sex" or "sexual variety," as men at least often say they are – although some women do want more excitement and romance. Women often feel more powerful emotionally in outside relationships because they cannot be taken for granted, they must at least be listened to, so that they won't leave.'

That women enter into extramarital affairs *primarily* for emotional, as opposed to sexual, reasons is further suggested by the *kind* of women who are most likely to have an affair, which is, perhaps, surprising. One might have thought that this huge increase in female infidelity would have taken place primarily among business women and professionals, who, working outside the home and as equals alongside their male counterparts, might fall in love with a colleague. But this is not the case. Studies show that it is specifically the women who do not work outside the home who are having more affairs; women who are financially dependent on their husbands and who may have fewer outlets to turn to in an emotionally unfulfilling marriage.

But perhaps the most significant indication that female infidelity is a response to an emotional vacuum, rather than a desire to have more sex, is the relatively low number of affairs among women – only 6 per cent – who are in love with their husbands and find their marriages emotionally fulfilling. The simple fact is that the overwhelming majority of women who claim to be loved by their husbands, and are shown that love, do not have extramarital sex.

It might even be argued that the cause of female infidelity is that women are no longer willing to stand for their husbands' affairs. Now that it is common for the women to be equal breadwinners for the family, they are not prepared to give a man love, obedience, and fidelity when he does not reciprocate. Women now put greater emphasis on what they are giving emotionally, so that they are more acutely aware when men do not return their affections. Women's increased social and economic independence means they are no longer prepared just to accept and put up with men's behaviour regardless.

One loyal wife, after discovering that her husband was having an affair with another woman, said, 'I am a social being – a human being with gifts to give and needs that have to be filled by other people. I'm beginning to think of looking outside our marriage for some of my affectionate needs.' And again: 'I think that if I do start seeing other people it will give me bargaining power, which I'm lacking. Many times I feel like he has all the power – makes most of the decisions and I just comply – which infuriates me.'

Similarly, another proclaims: 'I cheated on my husband after he shattered my world by cheating on me. I did it for revenge and also to be told I was pretty and wonderful, etc. – the romance. I felt terribly guilty afterwards and only truly loved my husband. I forgave him but he never truly forgave me. It had a damaging effect on our relationship, things were never the same.'

To be sure, there are many who militantly maintain that men and women have equally strong sex drives. They affirm that there are no sexual differences whatsoever between men and women, aside from physiology and plumbing. In *The Erotic Silence of the American Wife*, Dalma Heyn makes an impassioned argument for this position:

> *How often have we heard: women are by nature monogamous. Happily married women don't have affairs. Women do not desire a variety of sex partners. Women must love a man to have sex with him ... Women are not aroused by men's physical appearance ... Equally disturbing is the tendency on the part of some women to believe that while men really want sex, women*

> *want relationships. I question this: it is often*
> *a semantic distinction men and women are*
> *socially taught to make when in fact both may*
> *want both, and because it implies that sex is not*
> *an integral component of women's pleasure in*
> *relationships . . .*

I agree with Heyn that there are indeed many women whose powerful sexual urge is just like any man's. As a Rabbi to students, I know of several women who openly declare that they go into a relationship for sex only, just as male students may. But although there will always be exceptions to the rule, I believe we can generalise about male and female sexuality. I have met far more women who are interested in the totality of the relationship rather than the sex, and who indeed would not go to bed with a man whom they did not love. And all the statistics plainly show that in the overwhelming majority of cases, wives will not take a lover unless they feel unloved or ignored by their husbands. The same certainly cannot be said of men.

A wife taking a lover betrays a serious flaw in a marriage

It follows from this that female infidelity betrays a far more serious problem in a marriage than male infidelity. To be sure, male adultery is a serious violation of the marital vows, but a wife should not necessarily have to question her own desirability to her husband just because he feels attracted to other women. His promiscuous urges are natural, although they can and must be curbed, and he must focus his attention on his wife.

But if a wife loses interest in her husband, and begins to find love and romance outside the marriage, then the chances are that she is being ignored or marginalised by her husband, and this is serious indeed. Such a situation requires that a husband begin to respond to his wife's needs, and put her before everything else; he must make her feel that, in a world with roughly two and a half billion women, she is the most precious and the most special to him. If he doesn't then she will explore the terrain and find someone who does make her feel that way. I don't claim that this is simple; neither do I deny that there are women who are the exceptions to the rule and, like men, desire success with many different partners. But a husband who shows his wife extravagant love and affection has taken a huge step in the right direction.

It is the response to male infidelity that is more problematic. How does one reverse men's nature? Marriage begins to work against a couple. The more deeply they fall in love, and the closer they become and feel, the more familiar and comfortable they feel with each other as well. And the more familiar they become, the more the husband might naturally seek a new sexual partner affording plenty of mystery, adventure and novelty. One of the oddest things about adultery is the number of husbands who go to bed with women far less attractive than their wives. Why do they wander if they have a far more exquisite creature in their own beds? It is for the same reason that a woman will put on a brand-new dress she bought to go to a party, even though it is far cheaper than or inferior to a dress that has been sitting in the wardrobe for some time. It is the 'newness' that makes it attractive. We don't get excited about the nicest outfit we own, but about the newest. That's all there is to it.

What then is the cure for male infidelity? How can we assure the complete and undivided focus of a man's sexual attention and energy upon his wife? And how can a wife, and a husband, for that matter, always appear novel and exciting to their spouse?

4

Can we retain passion in marriage?

Once on a visit to Miami with my family, a few old classmates were kind enough to take me to a basketball game of Miami's new and very exciting team, the Heat. The game was entertaining and stimulating, and yet I was not focusing on the players or the ball. I could not take my eyes off a middle-aged couple sitting in the row right in front of me. During the entire evening this man did not take his arm off the shoulder of the woman he was accompanying. Even after he returned from buying some peanuts, he immediately sat down and his very first gesture was to put his arm back around her shoulder. When one of my friends, who held season tickets for seats in that row, saw me looking at them in wonderment, he bent over to me and said, 'For three years I have been coming to these games and for three years I have also watched in disbelief how this husband holds on to his wife throughout the game, every single moment. I promise you he does this every game and has never stopped. There is definitely something wrong.'

On the drive home from the game we debated between ourselves how this could be possible. How could this husband be showing such extravagant warmth to his wife? Not surprisingly, the conversation immediately turned into a discussion as to what could possibly be wrong with the man. One friend insisted that he must be having an affair with another woman, and overly compensating for it by showing his wife so much affection. Another friend suggested that they were not husband and wife at all but two lovers having an affair, albeit an indiscreet one, attending basketball games together for three years. This proposition was quickly rebutted by my friend with the season tickets, who knew the couple and verified that they were married. Another suggestion was that she was probably dying, and had very little time to live, and that was why her husband was being so kind and loving. What the exact explanation was I never found out, but the point is this: everyone in the car unanimously agreed that there must be something wrong with the man, because it is impossible to remain so loving in a marriage for so long.

Looking back it seems incredible! Not only have many of us lost the capacity to be at all times romantic and loving, and not only are we convinced that it is humanly impossible to sustain such love, we are even prepared to assassinate the character of those few odd couples who are totally romantically involved with each other, and posit the most sinister motives for their extraordinary behaviour.

But what *was* this couple's secret, and can we put it in a way that is easily accessible to us, and that we can apply to our own lives?

Sexual desire and desirability are all in the mind

As a religious individual, I have always rejected the prevailing religious thinking that all things physical are necessarily ungodly. This notion, promoted by most world religions, is not present within Judaism. The very first verse in the Bible reads, 'In the beginning the Lord created the heavens and earth,' implying that both were equally created by God, and thus both are holy and special; 'and God saw all that he had made, and it was good.' Understanding this is crucial. If physical existence is not special, and if it indeed represents the antithesis of things spiritual, then we must fight the fleshly desires of our human nature. But if human beings are holy, then human nature is commensurably holy. Rather than fighting human nature, we should harness it. Rather than reversing it, we must focus it. Rather than being ashamed of it, we must understand it and use it to our advantage.

The inclination for married people to look, even just glance, at other people outside the marriage for sexual possibilities, cannot be denied. Rather it must be respected and understood. Once we have analysed what is so downright exciting about the possibility of a new sexual partner, we must attempt to transpose that excitement into our marriages.

Let me relate the true story of a 42-year-old man and his 38-year-old wife. They got along fantastically well and felt themselves to be true companions. They trusted each other with every secret and comforted each other in their sadder moments. Only one major component was missing from their life together: passion. The husband accepted that this was primarily his fault. He loved his wife, but he no longer found her exciting. To be sure, he readily agreed that she was very attractive, and was told so on numerous occasions. But still, after 16 years of marriage, the novelty had worn off. It had been years since they had had a truly exciting intimate encounter. His lack of sexual interest was, of course, felt by his wife, and this led to a further deterioration of their marriage. The more she saw him looking at younger women, the more she began to crave attention from other men. And when he flirted openly with women at parties, she was positively enraged. The situation got worse and worse until they no longer even felt capable of discussing the matter. They reconciled themselves to the idea that their marriage provided stability, albeit at the expense of passion.

This deterioration led the husband to begin contemplating the possibility of having an affair. He thought that he might regain the lost excitement of early love in a mistress. He found himself eyeing many of his female co-workers, as if he were picking out a potential candidate. There were times when he was startled to find just how easy it would be to have an affair, and how many willing partners there seemed to be. Thoughts that had not been more than a passing fancy in his mind throughout all his years of marriage were now being entertained in great detail in his head. And there was an even more troubling development. Whenever he was in bed with his wife, he thought about other women. He simply felt the need to contemplate other women in order to find his sexual experiences with his wife exciting and satisfying.

But the husband noticed something. Whenever his *wife* stared at other men, or other men stared at her, or whenever he felt that she had a real interest in another man, he suddenly felt passionate about her once again. What were these deep dark emotions rising up within him? He knew that a sociologist would dismiss them as mere territorialism, but deep within himself he felt that this was more than just trying to reclaim what was rightfully his. Rather, he felt that he was once again viewing his wife as a *woman*, as a sexual being.

But what was he to do about developing this? Should he encourage his wife to have an affair and then tell him about it? He would not countenance such a thought. Besides, he knew that the kind of jealousy and hurt that would arise from such an experience would destroy him. He resolved to close his mind to that possibility. And yet he couldn't help feeling that the excitement of seeing his wife with another man might be the saving of his marriage.

He suggested to his wife that they go away on holiday together to the US Virgin Islands in an effort to spice up their withering love-life. There, they spent the first two nights together, but they still felt dissatisfied with their marital relationship. The husband then declared that they must take radical steps in order to resurrect their marriage. He presented his wife with a choice. Either she would agree to have a woman, presumably a prostitute, join them in a threesome, or else they would invite a man into their hotel room. He knew his wife would absolutely object to both of these options, so he told her that all he wanted was for her to agree to be massaged by a man in his presence. He also made it clear that while the masseur would not actually have sex with her, he might go a long way down that path. After much haggling and cajoling on his part, she reluctantly agreed.

The husband made a few calls in his wife's presence, and found a male 'masseur' who supposedly also had other specialities. It was arranged that the masseur, whose name was James, would come that night. The husband was surprised to find that his wife was actually showering, applying her make-up with care, and putting on her best lingerie in preparation for the experience. Just before the appointed hour arrived, the husband came up with a strange stipulation. He told his wife that she would have to wear a blindfold. 'I don't mind you being with this man,' he said; 'in fact, I know that you are doing it for me. But I don't want you to see his face. You simply can't see him, because then the experience would be too intimate.' His wife agreed that this was a good idea, saying that she would be far too shy if she had to look at him anyway.

But here came the twist. There was no James. The husband himself was to be James. He had already paid a hotel bellboy to call the room at 10 p.m. and announce on the phone to his wife that he was James and would be coming up. Next, the bellboy was to come up to the room, knock on the door, and announce himself as James the masseur. Earlier, the husband had bought new cologne which his wife would not recognise and an expensive wig that gave him shoulder-length hair. He had also devised a completely new sex routine.

When the appointed time came, he told his wife that he would sit in a corner while 'James' gave the massage, and asked if she was ready. She lay down, all the while with the blindfold on her face, and nodded. She was thoroughly fooled. He approached her and began to massage her back, slowly, patiently, and better than he had ever done before. He moved over every part of her body, paying more attention to detail than at any previous time in their married life together. He caressed and kissed her so that she felt as though he appreciated every part of her, and slowly she turned on like a light to a man who she thought was a complete stranger. Her husband continued to mix and match, trying and experimenting every way, in order to throw his wife off the track. He was thoroughly successful. His wife didn't have a clue. How could she? The man that she was married to had never treated her in this way before. 'James' was romantic and wonderful and found her vastly desirable. He lavished more attention on her in his intimate routine than her husband ever had.

After a full hour of touching, the husband became more ambitious. He knew his wife to be naturally shy, and was sure that she would resist his undressing her. But she did not. He took off every inch of clothing, and she did nothing to protest. Next, he began to go far beyond his mandate, and still she permitted him to go further. He held her hand softly, and she clasped his back. He kissed her passionately, and she kissed him back. In the space of three hours they shared full intimacy. His wife came alive like never before, and he began to wonder if she was indeed the same woman he had been married to all these years.

When the event was over, 'James', without saying a word, kissed the woman gently on the cheek and left. Her husband opened the door to allow him to depart, and then returned to his wife and removed the blindfold. His wife looked radiant and joyous. She thanked her husband for having organised the night, and told him how much she had enjoyed it. She also insisted on knowing whether or not he was upset, since things had far surpassed the original intention. He insisted that he was not, but deep down he felt a curious but immensely potent blend of passion and excitement mixed with shock and immeasurable hurt. His wife had in theory allowed herself to have sex with another man. Even though it had not really occurred, it had in her mind. He could never look at her in the same way again. The loving, caring, loyal and devoted wife whom he thought he knew had turned out to be none of those things. But on the other hand, the cause of his disappointment and anxiety was also the direct cause of his excitement and passion. Here he was married to such a passionate woman, such a sexual creature, that she would risk anything in the pursuit of physical pleasure. He now saw his wife in a totally new light. She was not just his wife. Indeed, she could not be fully possessed. She was a *woman*. And a sexy woman at that. A woman who had responded to the love and affection shown her by another man. Perhaps she would respond to her husband as well if he just tried a little harder.

For the next two days these antithetical emotions ran through his mind, driving him crazy. What did he want? A loyal wife or an exciting, adulterous wife? The passion he now felt for her, knowing what she had done, exceeded anything he had ever experienced before. He felt reborn, and his sexual relationship with his wife was unsurpassed. He now found her the most attractive woman in the entire world. So powerful was his attraction that he was not even tempted to look at the bikini-clad women on the beach, but instead gazed lovingly upon his wife the entire time.

But he was also scared. As far as his wife was concerned, she had had a much better time with another man than she had ever had with her own husband.

Would she therefore search for other men? Would she ever be satisfied with her own husband? When she closed her eyes at night during intimacy, who would she be thinking of: the dark mysterious man who had excited her but whom she had never seen, or the dull husband who was so uninteresting by comparison? In the end, he decided that he must tell her the truth, and he did. For her part, she could not, would not, believe it. At least not until he offered her all the evidence: the wig and the cologne.

Now, what had happened here? Why all the contrasts and contradictions? And how could they both have been so transformed by a single experience? Up until the moment when 'James' had started his massage the husband had seen his wife as all wife and no woman. He had become so accustomed to her that the novelty had worn off. He had not forgotten that she had passionate sexual needs but he had refused to accommodate those needs, focusing his energy instead on other women. Even though he was not actually unfaithful, he had forced her to assume a compliant and dull role. *She had no fire because he had snuffed it out.*

But the moment that she agreed to the bargain, he began to see her as a sexual creature, a fiery woman. A temptress. Playing the role of a possible suitor, he had to impress her, to win her over. He had given up trying to impress his wife long ago. Their intimate life had fallen into an unimpressive, yet acceptable routine. But here was a woman who was taking great risks to allow a paramour into her life. Moreover, he was supposed to be a professional. He had better be good! He would also have to try completely new things. Any element of their normal routine would expose him immediately.

For her part, she had been totally fooled, not really by the cologne and wig, but by the interest this man took in her, and the way he totally focused on impressing her. She was accustomed to a husband whose attitude in bed made her feel that he was bored by her. He was interested in younger and newer women. But 'James' was different. James genuinely liked and desired her. In fact, he desired her so much that he was willing to take risks for her, even to exceed his mandate and do something forbidden. And she came to life as a woman like never before.

I heard this strange tale when the wife, who was fairly religious and observant, came to me to ask whether or not she should repent. She wanted to know whether she had done anything wrong, since she hadn't actually committed adultery, although she had *thought* she had. After listening to the story, I went to her husband, who was a close friend, and questioned him about his motives, and the consequences of his actions. The results of the episode, according to him, are quite mixed. On the one hand, he swears till this day that he never thinks of any other woman when he is in bed with his wife. Nor does he need to. He insists that the mere memory of that night is enough to excite him for the rest of his days. He also insists that now he is far more passionate about his wife, and cannot forget what a sexy woman she is.

On the other hand, he has become far more insecure about his own standing. When he goes on business trips, for instance, he doesn't even contemplate having a fling with a new acquaintance, because his mind is far too occupied with what his wife might be up to. He finds himself thinking about her most anxiously, and telephoning her constantly to check up on her. He now knows that she is indeed capable of having an affair with another man. But is this really something negative? If the *possibility* of her being adulterous causes him to be totally absorbed in his wife and to think of her constantly, is it such a bad thing?

Adultery is destructive; the possibility *of adultery is beneficial*

I have always maintained, and shall continue to maintain, that the effects of adultery are entirely negative and destructive. They eat away at a marriage, and destroy the basis upon which it is built: trust and love. Still, what about the *possibility* of adultery? Can we not use to our advantage our recognition of the possibility that our spouse may be so driven sexually, and so desirable to the opposite sex, that at any moment they could betray all their marital vows and go off with someone else? If we live with this recognition, will it not lead us to a constant attraction to our partner, inspiring a real commitment to impressing them so as to retain their affections and concentration upon us, and thereby at the same time keep us from marital infidelity ourselves?

Adultery only arises where there is boredom, complacency and neglect. Only when a husband feels that he is dissatisfied, and that while he is running around his wife is safely at home minding the children, does he go about having an affair. Only when a wife feels that she is neglected while her husband spends all his time at the office does she look for someone new. Husbands and wives who are having affairs, when asked whether they think that their spouse is also having an affair, almost always respond that this is impossible. 'My husband? Forget it. He's just not the type. He's just not interested enough in sex to do something like this.' 'My wife has, I believe, never been "unfaithful" to me. Knowing her lack of interest in sex, I would be astonished to find out she had ever indulged herself elsewhere.' Of course, they often come in for a very rude awakening when they discover just the opposite. And when they do they feel flabbergasted and upset. But why? If they themselves are having an affair, why shouldn't their spouses?

The point is that if the average wife knew that her husband was the type to have an affair, then she never would have searched for a lover in the first place. Why should she? The loving passionate sexual firebrand that she was looking for was right here in her own bedroom. The problem is that he has never demonstrated it.

Sexual attraction is basically all in the mind. What you really need, if romance or passion is missing in your marriage, is not a new partner. *You need a new attitude*. And being made aware that your spouse is capable of having an affair causes you to see them in a completely new light.

The problem is how to achieve this awareness, and remember its lesson constantly. These are the methods that we are about to explore.

5

The Ten Commandments of adultery:

MAKING THEM WORK WITHIN MARRIAGE

'There can be no doubt that the lives of a very large proportion of married men and women are being enriched and made more meaningful by secret sexual relationships.'

Tony Lake and Ann Hills, *Affairs*, 1979

Mr Lake and Ms Hills may be right, but there are probably more people whose lives have been deeply scarred by extramarital relationships, families that have been destroyed, betrayed spouses who have utterly lost their self-confidence, and men and women who only wish that they could turn the clock back and reverse their adulterous liaisons.

Why did they do it? For a variety of reasons, but mostly excitement and rejuvenation; an end to the monotony of marriage. So what's the solution? If marriage and monogamy are doomed to lose their spark and become boring, but an affair betrays everything you believe in and can ruin your life, what are we to do? Give up? Submit to the inevitable loss of excitement in long-term relationships? Choose stability and permanence over passion, youth and vigour?

The answer is to have a secret, passionate sexual

71

relationship with your spouse. Turn your husband or wife into your lover. Make your marriage into a clandestine adulterous affair. Give your marriage all the ingredients that adultery has. Tap into its secret, and then bring all of its secret ingredients into your marriage.

So, what are those essential ingredients, and how can they work for you in your marriage? What does it take to have an exciting, illicit affair?

Essential ingredients for an adulterous affair

1. Adultery is first and foremost about sex. It makes each participant into a desirable sexual object

Yes, there are adulterous affairs that become deeply emotional and loving. But by and large adultery is about great sex and is entered into by both men and women who seek some spice in life, an end to their everyday routine, and a partner who really appreciates their bodies, treating them as if they are the most desirable person on earth. Adulterous affairs are not bogged down by problems of housework, cleaning, children and worries over finance. As the responsibilities of marriage increase, as bills pile up, as children are born, and as jobs become more demanding, often a couple's sex life is put on the back-burner. Everything else takes precedence and as a result their lovemaking suffers. An affair, however, is different. It is the essential sexuality of the man and woman involved that is accentuated – everything else is less important, or totally unimportant.

In Chapter 6 you will learn how to bring your sexual life with your spouse back to the foreground of your marriage, and to re-establish the centrality of lovemaking in your marital relationship.

2. Adultery thrives on separation and expectation

A large part of the emotional intensity of an adulterous affair is the constant waiting and yearning to be with your illicit partner. Since you don't want your spouse to catch you, you are living apart from your lover, always in a state of *expectation*. To an extent, you want what you can't have, and this is responsible for much the erotic excitement of adultery. Statistics show that adulterous partners who leave their spouses and move in together usually end up separating soon after. Once you get what you have been chasing, you're suddenly not so hungry any more.

In an adulterous affair, you think about your lover all the time, longing to be with them. Since you can't have sex with your lover any time you wish, you become obsessed with them and the sex you have with them. You try to compensate for the void by playing out the affair in your mind. You even tell yourself how you will make up the lost time by having the most wonderful sexual encounter upon your next reunion.

In Chapter 7 you will see how temporary periods of sexual abstention and separation can do wonders to reinvigorate your marriage.

3. Adultery thrives on a state of irreconcilable tension

The thrill of the chase, the fear of getting caught and not knowing when you'll next be able to see your lover all add to the excitement of adultery. These tensions keep the affair alive. You never have time to settle into a routine and stagnate. You are constantly on the move, setting up secret meeting places, tapping into your most creative resources to outsmart all those curious eyes around you, and to keep your affair going. It is a relationship that ultimately has no real solution, and thus it generates constant tension.

In Chapter 8 you will read how the natural attraction that even married people feel for other men and women outside the marriage, far from betraying the commitment of marriage, can ensure that we are constantly occupied with *choosing* our spouses anew. The anxiety caused by our natural inclination to promiscuity, set alongside our steadfast commitment to our spouse, guarantees that our marriages will never become stagnant or monotonous.

You will also learn how to use to your advantage the natural tension that exists between wishing our spouses to be seductive and hypnotic all round (which makes them attractive to others as well), and yet wanting to possess them entirely; and the intense feelings of jealousy stirred up by the glances that others might give them, and which they return.

4. Adultery thrives on secrecy, modesty, and mystique

I know it sounds strange, but yes, modesty. Part of the excitement of an adulterous affair is that only the two of you know about it. In life, things that are hidden always retain their lure, whereas things that have become too public are quickly forgotten. I know a man with a vast art collection, including Picassos and Van Goghs. At any given time, only one or two are on display in either his office or his home, because he wants them to remain precious in his and other viewers' eyes. Once a secret affair becomes known to the world, the excitement begins to dissipate.

In addition, those who are involved in adulterous affairs, however much we might condemn or despise them, carry with them an air of seductive mystique. Think of the great literary adulteress heroines: Tolstoy's Anna Karenina, Flaubert's Madame Bovary, Lawrence's Lady Chatterley, and Hawthorne's Hester Prynne. Being wanted by someone else in a sinful relationship bestows a certain erotic quality of mystery on a person.

In Chapter 9 you'll learn about the importance of modesty in marriage, and the harmful effects that sexual overexplicitness has wrought. You'll also learn how you and your spouse can alter your perception of each other to give your marriage an aura of secrecy, and how modesty will lead your spouse to cherish your body once more, and create an environment of mystery and intimacy.

5. Adultery involves intense focus

The points about separation, expectation, anxiety, secrecy, mystique and viewing your spouse as a total sexual partner together contribute to the real power of an adulterous affair: the complete sexual focus which one has on one's lover. Lovers who yearn for each other are not distracted by anything; they think only about each other. When they are in bed together, they do not feel the need to call up past images of other sexual partners to excite them. On the contrary, their passion is such that they are totally involved with each other and what they are doing at that moment. Not even thoughts about their marriage, security, or their children get in the way of their affair. *Too much about marriage is casual, whereas everything about adultery is intense.*

In addition, the risks lovers have taken to be together act as a catalyst to reveal their total sexual sides, and involve them in the relationship in a way unknown in marriage. United and impassioned by danger, they disclose their secret sexual fantasies to each other and let go of all inhibitions. In short, lovers in an illicit affair become magnets to one another, engaging each other's complete interest.

In Chapter 10 you will learn the secret of becoming a total sexual partner within marriage. You will discover the importance of sexual focus, the technique of making your spouse your only sexual outlet, and the immense passion and satisfaction this generates.

6. Adultery is about intense jealousy

The great majority of married women who enter into adulterous affairs do so not with single, but with married men. Thus, every time the couple separate after a rendezvous and return to their normal lives, the woman knows that her lover is going back to his wife, and she lives in a constant state of jealousy. She knows that she is the second woman in her lover's life, always a subordinate. When he goes on holiday, he does so with his wife and children, and indeed he spends most of his time in her company – and most of his nights in her bed.

In addition, since every act of adultery involves a betrayal of marital vows, the adulterer's lover is always aware that the person they are involved with is duplicitous. This person is always telling their spouse that they love them and that they are faithful, and then they leave their house to embark upon this double life. This knowledge that your lover is not faithful to his or her spouse leads you always to suspect that perhaps they are not faithful to you either. At the very least you know that they have the potential for betraying you, just as they have betrayed their spouse. This knowledge is painful, and stirs up feelings of jealousy. You know that you have no security – there is no home, children or even commitment to bind you – and thus you always fear being discarded in favour of someone else. Your lover may even choose to return to his or her spouse.

Your jealousy makes you want to possess your lover even more, so you exert every effort to sustain their attention. You always dress your best, speak lovingly, and are on your best behaviour.

In Chapter 11 you will learn about healthy jealousy and how indispensable it is in every marriage. Too many people complain that their spouses dressed better, spoke more kindly and treated them much better before they were married. You will discover how, if your spouse felt more jealous about you, their desire to possess you and their behaviour towards you would increase. You will learn that, in truth, no one has any real security in marriage and so you must devote great energy to earning your spouse's attentions.

7. Adultery is about trust

Sounds odd, doesn't it? But, even after everything I have said about jealousy, ironically and paradoxically adultery involves a large amount of trust. The adulterous party puts immense faith in their lover. They trust them not to tell anyone about the affair, unless they both agree on disclosure. They trust each other not to make their sexual encounter a one-night stand only. Let's face it, adultery involves terrible risks and can leave utter destruction – even suicide – in its wake. No man or woman is prepared to undertake these risks unless they feel they trust their partner to make the affair last, and not just to 'love them and leave them'. So great is the trust that a woman puts in her married male lover that although a startling 87 per cent of husbands who promise to leave their wives for their lovers do not in the end do so, still 82 per cent of the women who are promised this do believe it, and stay in the affair after an ultimatum has been issued to the effect of 'either leave your wife and move in with me, or I go packing'. It is this immense trust between adulterous partners that binds them, and makes them feel comfortably sexual with each other in their very precarious situation.

In Chapter 12 you will rediscover the centrality of loving trust in marriage, and the huge pay-off in closeness it brings. You will discover the benefits of *abstaining* from extramarital affairs, and how to re-instil truth, faith, and real companionship in your marriage, even after a spouse has been unfaithful. You will also learn how the faithfulness you show your partner by channelling your sexual energy in their direction actually serves as the single most powerful aphrodisiac, creating immense sexual – and erotic – passion.

8. Adultery is about attraction

Marriages today seem to be predicated primarily on compatibility and common interests. We are sexually attracted to and excited by the person we wish to marry, but we are perfectly prepared *not* to marry them if we feel that we don't have enough in common, if our communication is bad, our backgrounds are not similar, or if financial considerations are not favour-able. Of course, commonality of interests is important, but it is never as important as raw sexual attraction. It is this that keeps marriages together. People simply have to be interested in each other as individuals and not just in each other's *individual interests*. The mis-take of believing that *primarily* we must share things in common leads to the problem that, as time goes on, often the common interests begin to take precedence over sexual attraction, so that even though a couple may love going to the cinema together, enjoy the same kind of music, and read the same books, they can begin to drift apart.

Not so in adulterous affair, which is run entirely on the basis of attraction. Lack of common interests is subordinated almost entirely to the physical lure posed by that seductive member of the opposite sex. Many affairs begin with complete ignorance about the person in question: you go to bed with them not because they too love the opera, but because they make your skin tingle. In marriage we need to feel the same level of magnetism.

One of the most important things you will discover in Chapter 13 is the absolute centrality of physical and emotional attraction in marriage, and how real compatibility comes from the fact that you are one sex, and your spouse another, and not because you both love the opera. You will also learn how the power of physical attraction can be employed to your benefit in resolving marital strife.

9. Adultery boosts the ego; as such, it is an act of re-creation

As one woman quoted in the *Hite Report* said, 'The affair was wonderful for me emotionally. He was so powerfully attracted to me, thought I was beautiful.' Many people justify what they know to be a wrong move because of the need to feel rehabilitated after sharing their life with an uncaring, insensitive spouse.

The fact that someone else shows such an immense interest in you, coupled with their willingness to risk so much to enter into an affair with you, makes you feel once again as if you are the most desirable person on earth. When people are ignored or neglected, they feel as though they don't exist. An adulterous affair, for many people, makes them feel alive again, as if they were re-created.

Californian marriage and family counsellor Daphne Rose Kingman says that 'next to the death of a loved one, the ending of a relationship is the single most emotionally painful experience that any of us ever goes through'. In Chapter 14 I will show you how, instead of causing this pain, by focusing extravagant love on your spouse you can re-create him or her anew and bring novelty and freshness into your marriage.

10. Adultery is about passion, excitement, and newness

I saved the most important factor until last. Overwhelmingly, men enter into adulterous affairs simply because of the attraction posed by a new sexual conquest and a new body. The very *familiarity* of marriage can work against it, while the novelty of adultery has ensured that it has remained the most indulgent and erotic vice since the beginning of time. Just as we are always excited by buying a new car, or a new dress, adultery offers excitement by affording the opportunity for something new and different, while marriage offers more of the same.

But newness doesn't have to mean *acquiring*

something new. It can come in the form of rearranging the furniture of the house, re-upholstering that old sofa, re-spraying the car. It can also be achieved when you have lost an object, or thought you had lost an object, and find it again. What this affords is a new opportunity to rediscover what you already possess; to bring excitement and newness to those things you take for granted because, *to you*, they have become monotonous and boring.

Passion, excitement, and newness are not empirical concepts, but mental ones. They are all in the mind, and can therefore be easily induced with the proper techniques, as you will read in Chapter 15. The most important thing you will learn from this book is a proven method by which to constantly rediscover your spouse, guaranteeing more passion in your married life than you could ever experience with adultery.

What's this? Marriage, not *just as*, but *even more exciting than adultery*? Yes, *far* more. Read on and you'll see.

6

Becoming a total sexual partner

Adultery is first and foremost about sex. It makes each participant into a desirable sexual object.

My friend James was mortified when his wife Linda began scrutinising the Visa bills which kept on coming up with charges for 'Apparel' from an obscure place in Leeds. Her curiosity led her to telephone the bank and get the number of this strange establishment that had already cost them over £200. To her surprise a very seductive female voice picked up the phone on the other end. The stranger's first words were not the usual 'Hello,' but rather, 'What is *your* fantasy?' The number she had dialled was none other than a sex-talk line. Linda was flabbergasted that her husband would spend their precious funds on such nonsense, and she was personally insulted that he needed this. She felt humiliated and inadequate. Was talking about sex with another woman even more exciting than actually *having* it with his wife? she asked herself. He was too embarrassed to answer any of her questions. What did he talk about? she asked him. What was wrong with her that he felt he needed to have sex over a telephone? Her husband's silence infuriated her, and eventually they came to me for advice.

James refused to discuss the issue until his wife left

the office. Quietly, I persuaded her to do so. He then opened up. With an agonised look on his face he told me how Linda was a beautiful woman, but very squeamish, even shy, about sex. Yes, they could do it whenever they wanted. But they could never *talk* about it. He desired sexy talk with his wife, but she would always silence him. He wanted to know her fantasies, and wanted her to know his. Finally, in frustration, he began wasting their money on fantasy lines.

This story and countless others like it raise the subject of the extent to which today's husbands and wives are – or are not – sexually involved with each other, and the need to become a total sexual partner within marriage. Adulterous partners have established the sexual supremacy of their character over and above all other facets, something that is not always true in marriage. Husbands and their mistresses, wives and their lovers not only *have* more sex with each other, but think about it more, talk about it more, and expose their deepest darkest fantasies to each other. In her new autobiography, *Fear of Fifty*, Erica Jong relates how her current and third marriage seems to be succeeding where the others failed, and identifies one of the essential ingredients in preserving the sexual passion in the marriage as being her new habit of writing down and reading her sexual fantasies to her husband. One of the operative words in adultery is 'obsession', and adulterous partners are obsessed about each other constantly. How can we bring this into marriage?

Repression is always destructive but sexual focus is always productive

Judaism does not believe in repression. Of course, it is filled with restrictions regarding human behaviour. But whereas other religions restrict certain forms of human behaviour in their entirety, Judaism forbids certain acts in one area, but opens an arena for the performance of the very same acts in another. Judaism does not accept that anything is intrinsically evil. Rather, everything is neutral, that is, it has no innate good or evil quality. It is the objective of man to try to bring all these neutral elements into the camp of holiness. The Talmud proclaims that everything that God forbade in one area, He made permissible in another. Judaism does not seek repression of human nature, but rather a focusing and channelling of human nature so that it always expresses itself in a positive and productive way. There is no better example of this than sex and marriage.

Judaism's most notable prohibitions are those against adultery, homosexuality and incest, which are seen as ungodly activities. But sex itself is not ungodly. On the contrary, used correctly it serves as the ultimate statement of human love and closeness emulating the celestial union of the masculine and feminine aspects that exist within the Godhead itself, as explained at length in Jewish mysticism. Whether or not sex is moral and holy does not depend on the sex act itself, but rather on how humans go about doing it. For instance, even in marriage sex can be unholy, such as when a spouse thinks about someone else while in bed, or when a husband has sex with his wife against her consent, an activity strictly prohibited by Jewish law.

If you walk through the woods and find a stick,

either you can use the stick to build a fire and give yourself and perhaps others warmth, or you can bang someone on the head and rob him of his possessions. The object is itself neutral. The use to which it is put is not. The same is true of sex. In God's kindness He gave us the most passionate and exciting way in which to bond with another human being in pleasure and holiness, thereby expressing our love for them. How we use or abuse this special opportunity is our choice. If we choose to squander our sexuality the only ones to suffer will be ourselves.

In one of the most liberal and significant statements of any ancient religious text, the Talmud states, in summing up the sexual practices that are allowed between a husband and wife, 'In the final analysis, a husband and wife can do whatever pleases them most,' meaning they should pursue sexual practices that excite them. The great many verses in the Bible dedicated to sexual prohibitions, with the exception of having sex during menstruation, virtually all apply to extramarital sex, not to sex between a husband and wife. There can be no greater illustration of the advanced Jewish outlook on sex, nor a better expression of how Judaism believes not in repression, but in focus and sublimation. The same activities that are absolutely prohibited with another man or woman become not just permitted, but holy, when done with one's husband or wife.

What humans desire is not just sex, but to be sexual

Far from being merely the act of coitus, human sexuality is humankind's most instinctive impulse.

But humans do not merely need or desire to have sex. Rather, they have a desire to *be sexual*. They need to think sexy thoughts, speak about and indulge in erotica, look at sexy things and undertake sexual acts. The best kind of sex is that which consumes us entirely. This is why premarital sex, where you are conscious of being judged according to your performance, can never have the fulfilment of marriage where you feel completely relaxed and natural with your spouse. Sexuality is not an ancillary dimension of human existence. Rather it is a total statement of what people are and what they do. If a husband and wife are to be happy together, it is essential that they serve as a *total sexual outlet* for each other. Don't ever give your spouse the excuse of having to find erotic outlets outside the marriage.

I know of a husband who had a kind and loving relationship, and a very active sex life, with his wife, yet still ended up committing adultery on a number of occasions, which resulted in his wife leaving him. So why did you do it? I asked him. He told me, 'Well, it started when I began calling phone-sex lines. I would often ask my wife very personal questions about how she felt about sex in an effort to have an erotic conversation. But she was extremely shy on the subject. I would ask her if she used to masturbate before we married, and she would turn red and change the subject. Well, one thing led to another, until I no longer felt she was a complete sexual partner. She's a great woman, but very reserved and thus cannot supply me with all my sexual needs. There are things which I just need to find outside the marriage.'

This of course is in no way a proper justification for

adultery, and this husband was a fool for betraying his devoted and loving wife. Nevertheless, the story does provide an important lesson. Sex and marriage are at their best when a husband and wife are sexual together in every possible way. This is the essence of adultery and the secret of successful illicit lovers: they always put sex first. A husband and wife should endeavour to destroy or transcend any sexual inhibitions that separate them and to become a complete sexual outlet for each other. Refraining from an adulterous affair, but not involving your total sexual self in your marriage, is not enough. You will still be losing the opportunity to use sex to its utmost in binding you and your spouse together.

To be sure, nobody has the right to demand that their partner instantly submit to their every sexual need, especially when the other is uncomfortable with certain activities. Rather, they must try to show their partner how important this might be to them, how it would benefit their marriage, and how it would assist in making them even more of an exclusive sexual partnership, strengthening their love. One's spouse should not be seen as one's business partner, housemate, best friend, psychiatrist, and, in addition to all these things, *also* one's partner for sex. Rather, a spouse must be first and foremost one's lover. Everything else is subordinate.

Remember the first rule: if our husbands and wives are totally absorbed with us sexually, if they can talk about sex with us, fantasise about sex with us, look forward to sex with us, plan the most exciting sexual encounters with us, and actually go ahead and have it all with us, then there is no reason in the world that they should have to look for sex outside marriage. It is when a husband and wife make everything else in their marriage more important than sex that one of them is likely to stray.

What form does this straying take? Why, in finding a lover for the almost exclusive purpose of sex. The primary attraction of taking a mistress or a paramour is that one focuses together with them on sex almost entirely, something that was not happening at home. Although a couple might have children together, buy each other beautiful clothes and jewellery, this still does not serve as a replacement for the primary purpose of marriage, nor, therefore, will it safeguard against the possibility of adultery.

Marriage is too important not to come first

How sexy a husband or wife feels depends largely on their spouse. A husband should never feel the need to look at *Playboy* in order to see a woman in a certain item of lingerie or a certain position. A wife should never have to switch on a film to hear a man tell a woman poetically how beautiful or special she is. The moment a man sees a sexy piece of lingerie on a mannequin in a store, if it excites him, he should buy it on the spot, and fit his wife into it. Similarly, if a woman finds a particularly romantic novel inspiring, about a couple's trip to Venice, for example, she must persuade her husband to hop on a plane at their first available opportunity so they may enjoy the experience together. Go ahead and fantasise. But fantasise about your wife. Better yet, translate the fantasy into reality by living out your dreams – together.

You may argue that this advice is impractical – you

can't just drop everything and take off somewhere at a moment's notice. But I ask you this: if you were at work and heard that the plumbing at your house went haywire and was flooding all the rooms, would you not run home immediately? Well, why don't we do the same thing in marriage? When our home is in danger of physical destruction, we move heaven and earth to protect it. But when our marriages are in danger of dying a horrible death of monotony and boredom, we are all too often *too busy to save them*. Our marriages are the most important things in our life, and we should, if we have to, accept ridicule, financial loss and even sacrifice our careers to boost and salvage them.

In an adulterous affair, you would be forced to find the time in the middle of the workday to run to hotel rooms, and the like, in order to secretly spend some time with your lover. Why should marriage be any less spontaneous? If we can find the time to run around behind our spouse's back, why can we not find time to run around *with* our spouse?

Discuss sexual fantasies with your spouse

By telling your spouse your sexual fantasies, you make them become a total sexual partner to you. And by hearing them from you, they begin to see you as a sexual being who is creative and imaginative, and they will grow excited with you again. You should be able to relate your fantasies to each other, and dress up in accordance with each other's wishes. It may seem strange at first, but with time you will find it easier, and the intimate passion and closeness in your marriage will increase immeasurably.

7

Sexual separation in marriage

ADULTERY THRIVES ON SEPARATION AND EXPECTATION

*'The time away [from his wife] had a
salubrious effect on their marriage and each
visit home was a renewed honeymoon . . .
after seeing the children, they made love
with a fervor reminiscent of their courtship.'*

Gay Talese, *Thy Neighbor's Wife*

Ready and willing for sex

I discovered the expression 'ready and willing for sex'
from a Jewish husband whose wife, together with
him, was studying more about Judaism and desired to
become more observant. They had been married for
five years, and from their conversation it was clear
that much of the spark of their marriage had gone
(he started frequenting a health club and his wife
said jokingly that she didn't mind him getting running
lessons from the big-chested woman in the tight leotard
because 'it would be a miracle if he got excited about
anything these days'). I suggested to them that they
could kill two birds with one stone.

One of the central tenets of Jewish family living is
what are known as the Jewish laws of family purity.
The Bible stipulates that once a month, for the five
days of normal menstruation, and for seven nights

91

thereafter, a husband and wife should not engage in intimate relations. This precludes not only having sex, but even hugging or sleeping in the same bed (because one thing leads to another). Thus, for 12 days a month, a husband and wife live in physical separation. At the conclusion of this interlude, the wife goes to a *mikveh*, or Jewish ritual bath, the water of which is drawn from and always connected to a living spring, for immersion, after which she reunites sexually with her husband.

As every husband and wife who have been separated from one another for two weeks should already know, the sexual reunion that follows is explosive. As your wife comes home from *mikveh* and enters the bedroom, you literally rip each other's clothes off. What separation does is repackage our old lovers as new. And although I do not believe that this is a complete solution to the problem of how to restore lost passion in marriage, it is undeniable that observing the laws of Jewish family purity is extraordinarily effective. Many a Jewish author has described the monthly night of reunion as 'a second honeymoon every month', and this it really is. I therefore advised this couple that if they wished both to become more observant and instantly to re-instil passion into their marriage, they should observe a monthly period of sexual abstention.

The reason that separation is only an incomplete and temporary solution to restoring passion in marriage is self-evident. It avoids dealing with the root of the problem. Its implication is that a husband and wife can never sustain a passionate relationship, and must therefore go without being together for a while, in order that they should look forward to their reunification. The loss of sexual interest in one's spouse is a problem in mental perception, not in reality, and must first and foremost be addressed in the eye of the mind.

After this woman had been to the *mikveh* for the first time, I asked her how she viewed the experience. 'It really was amazing,' she told me, 'and it made me feel the sexiest I've ever felt. For two weeks I didn't, and knew that I couldn't, have sex. Then, I went to *mikveh*, and afterwards, before going home, I put on my prettiest dress and most beautiful make-up, and underneath it all I wore my sexiest lingerie – all for my husband's benefit. I had to stop on the way home to fill the car with petrol. I could tell that all the men at the petrol station couldn't take their eyes off me. I felt that I was very desirable. But I could also tell that the reason wasn't only the way I was dressed. Rather, it was the way I felt about myself, and how I carried myself. After having been off limits for nearly two weeks I was ready and willing for sex. I was a woman who felt very sexy, and everybody noticed. I wasn't at all flirtatious and wasn't dressed immodestly. And I didn't have to be. The men noticed me none the less. When I got home to my husband, we had the most memorable night of our marriage. I told him how all the men on the way home had looked at me, and my husband saw the same thing. I felt he really wanted me.'

Abstention and separation lead to the build-up of sexual energy

Human nature innately needs separation in order to thrive and flourish, and the love between husband and wife, being fiery as opposed to watery, operates on heightened moments of passion, with intermediate moments of lessened passion. So even if your marriage is not always passionate, that's all right and there's no real reason to panic. Marriage needs hills and valleys, and not everything can appear new all the time. There is nothing to worry about if half the time you find your marital relations more calm, as long as for the other half they are passionate. The two abstemious weeks of a month actually strike a very good balance in contrast to the two more fiery, sexual weeks. They serve as periods when a couple can develop the non-sexual dimension of their relationship, especially their communication. But if you go more than two weeks a month without at least a strong breeze if not an outright earthquake, you must do something urgently and refer to the other suggestions in this book. It is very difficult to abstain from sex with your spouse, let alone not share the same bed. But the benefits really are immensely rewarding.

It is possible to induce a perpetual state of expectation, of the same kind that keeps adulterous affairs alive and exciting, with your spouse, even though you share the same house and the same bed nightly. If you are Jewish, I strongly recommend that you begin to observe the laws of sexual abstention in their entirety and not only separate, but go to *mikveh* after the 12-day separation period is over. The actual laws that govern this period are easy to follow, and many short guides about them have been produced (the best are *Waters of Eden* by Rabbi Aryeh Kaplan and *A Hedge of Roses* by Rabbi Norman Lamm). If you are not Jewish, I suggest that you institute a period of abstention and separation in your marriage for at least the five days (upon average) of menstruation and for as many days thereafter as possible, up to a week. Try to keep it up for as many days as you can, up to seven. Many women in any event express a feeling of discomfort, even humiliation, about having sex while they are having their periods. I'm aware that most couples will not go so far as to move out of the marital bed (as the laws of family purity demand). But still, in this period of sexual abstention you must really abstain, and that means from any form of sexual release, not just coitus. Allow your sexual 'steam' to build up. Don't engage in any form of oral sex, don't masturbate, and don't look at pornographic magazines or films with explicit sexual imagery. Let yourself become an obsessed sexual being who thinks about your spouse constantly, and wishes finally to release all that pent-up sexual desire with him or her.

You will also find that you treat your spouse far more kindly and argue less during this period of pent-up sexual excitement. Closing off all other sexual outlets, allowing your sexuality to build up, and knowing that the only person with whom you can release this powerful build-up is your spouse will lead to a real feeling of dependency. You need your spouse. You think about them always. You long for that fantastic night of reunion which is just a few days away.

In films we hear constant jokes about how men who have been in prison, or who have been prisoners-of-war for many years, react upon seeing their first woman. To them, she is an enchanted princess, irrespective of how she compares with other women. They have not had a sexual partner for many years, and they have a powerful lust for this one woman who is now before them as if she were a goddess. I have a close

Mormon friend who, true to the traditions of the Church, never had sex until his wedding night, which wasn't easy since he married at 33. The wedding was to take place in California, and his student friends at Oxford all joked that the Californian authorities would prohibit him from conducting the wedding there for fear that he and his bride, who was also a virgin, might displace the San Andreas fault and have the whole state fall into the Pacific. Well, you can make your wife into that same enchanted princess by following these easy steps. Remember:

- Abstain from all forms of sexual contact for a period of between five and 12 days per month.

- During this period refrain from any other form of sexual outlet or gratification, including and especially masturbation.

- Plan your night of reunion in a special hotel, or send the kids to friends, or go away for the weekend. Every month you will be guaranteed not just another wedding night, but a good few days of the most exciting and passionate sex.

8

Attraction to strangers keeps marriage vibrant

ADULTERY THRIVES ON A STATE OF IRRECONCILABLE TENSION

'Nobody bothered to tell you what marriage was really about . . . You expected not to desire any other men after marriage. And you expected your husband not to desire any other women. Then the desires came and you were thrown into a panic of self-hatred. What an evil woman you were! How could you keep being infatuated with strange men? How could you do that to your husband? Did anyone ever tell you that maybe it had nothing to do with your husband?'

Isadora speaking to herself in
Erica Jong's *Fear of Flying*

Amazingly, one of the greatest hopes for reinvigorating marriage with newness and freshness comes from the very side of human nature that is directly responsible for adultery: our attraction, even after marriage, to strange men and women. Is it wrong, then, for a husband or wife to be attracted to other people? To an extent, the question is irrelevant. It is simply a fact that even while we are fully and utterly in love with and devoted to our spouse, this does still not preclude us from noticing other men and women, and at times harbouring a strong attraction to them.

Loyalty of the mind

Does it betray a lack of love for one's spouse if one feels attracted to other people, without ever acting upon such interest? I am not asking whether it is reasonable for one to notice the fact that other people are attractive, which is absolutely normal and to be expected. Rather, is it acceptable to allow oneself *to be attracted* to other men or women besides one's spouse? Is it excusable if one's flesh heats up as a result of pondering the sexuality of someone outside the marriage? Is it acceptable to *want* to commit adultery, so long as one never actually does it, always remaining faithful in practice?

One of the most frequent complaints that wives voice is that when their husbands take them out, often they cannot focus their attention on their wives, but instead pay heed to every pair of legs that passes them by. For it's true: a man may enjoy a wonderful relationship with his wife, but this does not mean that he is not attracted to other women, sometimes strongly so, even while he is in the company of the woman he loves.

This behaviour is of course unacceptable, and wives justifiably find it insulting. And I strongly maintain that men must do their best to transcend their natural attraction to women, and women to men, and focus their sexual interest on their spouse. Yet our attraction to others is an undeniable and potentially hurtful phenomenon, and warrants closer scrutiny. It seems almost unfair, that although we can be so totally in love with our spouse, we are still so aware of the sexual appeal of others. Why is this, and how can it be used to our advantage in marriage?

The tension between good and evil

To answer this question, we must digress briefly and explore the nature of good and evil in Jewish thought. Those people who endeavour to lead good, righteous lives will notice that even if they have overcome the struggle to perpetrate an evil or dishonest act, it becomes no easier to choose good the next time round. It is just as difficult, and the same effort is required on each and every occasion. It is possible that choosing the right thing may become marginally easier with the passage of time, and indeed the great medieval Jewish thinker Maimonides maintained that man has two natures, the first being innate, and the second acquired through repetitive action. The more often you do something good, even amidst fierce inner resistance, the easier it becomes to repeat the act, until it actually becomes second nature. And yet the struggle will always remain. Life is not easy, and doing the right thing always is certainly not easy.

So why it is so difficult just to be a good person and to choose goodness on every occasion? Why can't we make one choice at the age of 12 or 13 to lead a good life, and remain that way for the rest of our lives? Why must these choices be made continually? Why did God make it all so difficult?

The Zohar, the most fundamental work of Jewish

mysticism, provides the answer: whenever good is chosen over evil, the glory of God is raised infinitely higher. This means that Judaism does not believe in man making one choice of good over evil which lasts for ever. What God desires is not *righteousness*, so much as the *struggle* to do the right thing: a daily struggle to choose good over evil, God over wickedness, charity over selfishness, compassion over being judgemental, love over hate, and fidelity over adultery. The reason is that God is glorified far more if good is chosen repeatedly rather than just once; it is a far greater statement of a love for goodness if it is chosen constantly and consistently. *Choosing goodness must be a daily activity*, not something confined to our past. If we had the capacity to choose to follow a righteous path once and for all early in our life, then God would not be playing an active role in our lives. He would be associated with an ancient decision we made in our youth, and which we have not thought of since. Instead, we are afforded an opportunity to bring God and goodness into our daily lives and make His presence felt in a meaningful way.

Marrying every day of our lives

In a similar vein, we may say that the reason that God created us in such a way that we feel attracted to other men and women, notwithstanding our love for and loyalty to our spouse, is so that we have the opportunity to express the most sublime level of love: that which comes about through *constant choice*. We cannot rely on a one-off statement made under the wedding canopy for our fidelity. Rather, our commitment is dynamic, constantly being reinforced and strengthened. Far greater than a past statement of love and choice is a statement says, 'I love you and choose you ceaselessly. Not just once, long ago, but every single day.' This kind of love is dynamic and fresh, rather than stale and old.

The only person in the world

A wife might consider it a great compliment if her husband said to her, 'You should know that I am not at all attracted to other women; I don't even notice them, only you. It is not even that you are the most beautiful woman to me, it is simply that you are the *only* woman as far as I am concerned.' But far more flattering would be the proclamation, 'There are many very beautiful, attractive women whom I have encountered. And to be honest, I find them appealing and desirable. And yet I have chosen to be with you, because to me you are the most special, and nobody can compare to you. In a world of beautiful and attractive people, you are the *most* beautiful.' Such a statement, instead of making your wife feel that you love her because she is akin to being the only woman on a desert island, and essentially you have no choice but to love her, makes her feel rather that she has won a contest and is the most desirable woman, amidst some very stiff competition.

When a woman remains steadfastly loyal and in love with her husband, despite finding other men attractive, he can really feel special. He is not *alone*, but rather he is *unique*, in a class of his own. He understands that his life with his wife is not something stale or in the past. She loves and chooses him *constantly*. Choosing one's spouse constantly expresses the depth and intensity of the relationship. The most sublime way of telling someone 'I love you' is 'I have *chosen* to make you mine, and I go on choosing you daily. I am never complacent about my love for you and my need to *do* something about it.'

If a husband and wife, separated by a business trip, were to find no necessity to struggle to remain faithful in heart, mind and deed to each other, what would this say about their marriage? Of course, it would mean that their marriage is very secure, but not passionate and alive. They got married long ago and now find no need to invoke the memory of each other while away in order to remain faithful, since they are not at all tempted by anyone else. But the husband or wife who naturally feels an attraction to a business associate to whom they are not married, in order to remain faithful must have recourse to the loving memories of their loyal spouse waiting for them at home, and thus they take their spouse and their marriage with them everywhere. This requires no small effort, but the rewards are great: the result is a marriage of the highest quality within which one's spouse is continually affirmed as being chosen, rather than merely being established once and for all as 'the wife' or 'the husband' and taken for granted from that point onwards. This is a beautiful insight into relationships which one may cull from Jewish religious thought.

9

Bored with sex: the loss of passion in relationships

ADULTERY THRIVES ON SECRECY, MODESTY, AND MYSTIQUE

'I am happy now that Charles calls on my bedchamber less frequently than of old. As it is, I now endure but two calls a week and when I hear his steps outside my door I lie down on my bed, close my eyes [ready myself for sex], and think of England.'

Lady Alice Hillingdon, *Journal* (1912)

A couple whose wedding ceremony I conducted invited family and close friends to their beautiful bridal suite in the elegant Claridge's Hotel for drinks after their wedding reception. After about an hour, I started saying in a loud voice, 'Boy, is it late, and am I tired! I guess we'd all better be going now.' And turning to one of the guests, I said, 'Aren't you coming, too?' People began to take the hint. It was, after all, this couple's wedding night, and we all had to scram. But just as everybody was leaving, the bride, who was very beautiful, began to cry: 'Oh, please don't go yet. I can't believe the wedding is over.' Her new husband tried to comfort her. 'What's wrong, darling?' With tears rolling down her cheeks, she said, 'I don't want to take off my wedding dress.' Of course, she meant that she loved being a bride and couldn't believe that the most special moment of her life was now over. But how do you think her husband felt hearing this? You see, this couple had been living together for two years prior to the wedding. They separated just one day before the wedding. How new or special was their wedding night going to be?

One of the greatest fallacies ever advanced in the history of human relationships is that people simply cannot become bored with sex. Here, I don't only mean bored with the same sexual partner; I mean bored with sex in general. Ours is such an oversexed society that we think we can never get enough of it. But this is a far cry from the truth. People are becoming increasingly bored with sex.

Recently, two students who had been going out together for over half a year, and who seemed to be quite serious about their relationship, broke it off abruptly. As I am quite friendly with them, they candidly told me when I asked why it had petered out, 'We quite literally screwed the life out of our relationship. We had sex at every possible moment, several times a day. It's just not exciting any more. We don't seem to have much more to look forward to.'

All around the world, the jury is back and the verdict is in: people are getting bored with sex. From magazines to movies, flesh and erotica are out, while dressing and subtlety are back in fashion. In Britain the porno magazines are dressing their models in order to sell copies. The *Sunday Times* reported that *Penthouse* magazine, 'the men's magazine that was the first to bare all, is asking its models to put their clothes back on. Skin, it seems, is no longer "in".'

What has led to this sudden exercise in modesty?

Could it be the Christian 'decade of evangelism', or the Jewish call for a 'decade of renewal'? Is it a general return to a more puritanical era and ethos? No, nothing quite as profound as that. It is simply a business decision. The *Sunday Times* went on to say, 'The plunging sales of "girlie" magazines have led to a catharsis in Britain's publishing industry ... *Penthouse* once boasted 500,000 readers; now it claims 120,000 a month ... The number of naked women is being reduced in favour of serious features ...' They feel that they will actually gain more subscribers if they dress their models with clothes ... Is this possible? This is a pornographic magazine, isn't it? Can someone please tell me just what the heck is going on?

At the outset of the sexual revolution, it was assumed that the more sex poured into a society, and the easier sex became to obtain, the greater the interest would be. Of course, this ran completely contrary to everything we know about every other area of life. It is specifically the scarcity of things that makes them precious. If the streets were lined with diamonds they would be worth no more than granite. Sex, like so many other areas of life, can suffer from overkill. Yes, ladies and gentlemen, the unthinkable is true: people can become just as bored with sex as they can with anything else.

Casual sex

Society has become so complacent about sex. Its explicitness has caused sex to lose its mystique. A wife catches her husband with another woman and he apologises, but cannot understand why she is so hurt.

'It was just sex. I didn't love her.' Just sex! *Just* sex!! Yes, just sex. Because sex has become totally casual, and therefore a husband can equate it with washing a woman's car. Nothing serious in that either.

One of the great challenges of modern-day living is to re-establish the parameters that separate the casual from the intense. Life needs centres of intensity. Human undertakings must be understood not as casual and arbitrary, but as purposeful and meaningful. It is purpose that makes things passionate and intense. When you acquire money unearned, or accidentally, such as by winning a lottery, you are never as respectful of that money as you would be if it had come through hard work. If a man or woman truly believed that their spouse was chosen for them by heaven, and that their marriage was preordained, they would be very passionate about making it work. But today, when so many people speak of having accidentally married the 'wrong' person, how can they be excited about making their marriages special? Lack of purpose sucks out the intensity from our marriages and makes them casual. Our attitude becomes, 'If it works out, then great. And if not, then there's always something or somebody else.'

I met a student who was very intelligent, but also slightly immature. He was 18 years old and had been very sheltered by his mother. He came to the L'Chaim Society on Friday nights and became very friendly with a girl. They used to go for drinks and to plays together and eventually started going to her room and talking late into the night. This happened numerous times, but he was naive about the ways of the world and didn't quite comprehend that there was something romantic happening. He thought it was just a friendship until one night when, in the middle of a conversation about a film they had seen, the girl began to unbutton her blouse right in front of his eyes.

The student came to me the next day as white as a sheet. I asked him what had happened to make him look so grim; did a relative die, God forbid, or did he lose his best friend? He answered no, something far worse. Almost in a daze, he said, 'I always dreamed what it would be like to be with a woman for the first time, it was something mysterious and inviting, which I very much looked forward to. Last night it was all stolen from me. When for the first time a young woman undressed in front of me, it was in a totally casual way. I believed that it was going to be passionate, electric, exciting, intense. It ended up being almost accidental. She did it for me, but it didn't feel natural.' Then in a most uncharacteristic display of anger, he pounded his fist on the table and shouted, '*It was so damn casual!*' He felt that he had been cheated, and that the line that separates the casual from the intense had somehow been blurred that evening. And the first truly intense experience that he was meant to have had become something commonplace, as if nothing special had happened.

Modesty preserves intimacy

Judaism has long advocated the need for modesty in society: in the way people dress, the way they speak, even the way they think. While many thought that the purpose of the laws concerning modesty was to prevent sinful thoughts, they were wrong. Modesty is necessary to *preserve intimacy*, not to prevent sin. There is an old question, 'Do you lock your house to keep people out, or to protect what is on the inside?' Similarly, should a person act and dress modestly in order to prevent intrusion from outside, or to preserve what is inside: the precious ability to maintain an intimate relationship?

An intimate moment is one when two individuals invite each other into their private space. Not just a private room, but *a private part of themselves*. If every bit of ourselves has already become public property through lack of modesty, what part of us remains preserved for an intimate moment? Today's lack of emphasis on modesty has meant that our intimate selves have become like a secret told to too many people. It still may be exciting news, and a lot of people may be interested in hearing it until it gets stale. But in no way is it personal or private. The human body is meant to be explored within marriage. That is what makes the body a treasure instead of a public playground.

Explicitness kills romance

In an earlier generation there were many expressions of love outside the bedroom. This was the meaning of romance. A couple would hold hands, dance together or cuddle. In today's society non-involved men and women kiss and hug even as a form of greeting, and total strangers dance together at parties: what is left to a couple as an expression of affection besides the bedroom? And we are quickly becoming desensitised even to that.

While in Amsterdam with my family for a weekend,

I wondered whether in this, probably the most sexually explicit city in the world, people's sense of romance had been deadened. I observed the people in the street for hours on end, searching continually for couples who were holding hands. Did the romantics still exist? I saw only five. I was hardly surprised. Why would something as simple yet romantic as holding hands have any excitement in a city where one can see exposed flesh in every shop-front? Why waste time on petty romance when you can go straight for the kill and immediately have sex? When the threshold of excitement is constantly lifted, we soon become immune, even where male and female sexual organs are concerned. In Amsterdam, men sit in bars watching women perform the most explicitly sexual acts with not a stitch of clothing on. And are they excited about it? No! *They are bored to death.* They turn away to order more beer and start talking about business or sport again.

A recent article in *Newsweek* magazine told of a long-running French nudist colony which was now undergoing a rebellion by its young. Many of the founding members of the colony were troubled that they were not able to impart their tradition of naturism to their children. One of the girls explained why, unlike her parents, she was wearing a bathing suit on the beach: 'If I don't put on clothes,' she said, 'the boys don't even look at me.' Many of my American friends who come to the topless European beaches, which are outlawed in the United States, feel the same way. For the first few days their attention is caught by every mammary gland that passes. After a few days, however, skipping stones on the surface of the sea becomes more interesting. Seeing a person partially hidden from view can be far more exciting than seeing them openly displayed. It is modesty that makes intimacy possible.

Don't let your sexual steam leak out

In his book *Doesn't Anyone Blush Anymore?*, Manis Friedman tells this steamboat story. Soon after the steamboat was invented, a captain brought his boat down a river and stopped at a small village in Europe to show it off. He was fascinated by his new toy, and tried repeatedly to impress the simple peasants with the loud boom of his foghorn. Over and over again, the captain stoked the engines, got up a big head of steam and sounded the horn. But when the time came to show how the boat ran, it wouldn't budge. He had used up all his steam on the foghorn.

If we waste our sexual energy wherever we go, letting it leak out wherever we roam, we are left without any when we need it. If we are sexual when it doesn't count, we will have no steam left when it does. If we dress in an explicit and provocative way when we are not in a sexual situation, then our bodies may not pose the same erotic attraction necessary later to create a sexual situation.

According to Jewish thought, a healthy society is one that is completely alert sexually, and knows that if women *and men* don't dress modestly, they will soon become desensitised and less attractive to one another. If men and women, whilst socialising and being a part of the outside world, put up a curtain that separates their inner selves from everyone else, they will be able, at other times, to life that curtain to allow someone else to enter their private space for intimate purposes.

Overexposure dulls passion

I was sitting with a couple whom I did not know all that well, at whose wedding I was to officiate in Oxford. I told them that Jewish law advocates that husband and wife dress and act modestly with each other. If you are not preparing for a sexual or intimate encounter, a wife should be wearing a nightgown and the husband pyjamas, not always parading around the bedroom nude.

Nothing upset the prospective bridegroom as much as that comment. He was furious that I was telling them how to conduct their private lives and found this very offensive. He was prepared to accept that Judaism had the right to make demands on our public lives. But to encroach upon people's private lives was absolutely wrong. I responded, 'Look, you can discard this advice and insist, as you have been, that how you conduct your intimate married life is your business only, and no one has the right to offer any advice. But by doing this, you run the risk of the nightmare scenario. You are so exposed to each other's bodies for such long periods of time that one day your wife will arrive home, you will be reading the newspaper, she will undress and you will *still be reading the newspaper*.'

Judaism insists that husbands and wives don't parade around each other naked, not for any puritanical reasons, but so that they don't become bored with each other. Overexposure leads to dullness. Modesty, on the other hand, leads to newness, discovery and the ability to be excited about the subject.

Modesty, therefore, is one of the principal avenues by which we can turn our marriages into illicit affairs. One of the great secrets of adultery is that two lovers never grow bored with each other since they are never overexposed to each other. They don't live together or share the same bedroom and they only undress in front of each other when they wish to have sex. Thus, they always cherish each other's bodies. In marriage it should be no different, with husbands and wives choosing to undress only with the intention of creating moments of passion and intimacy.

10

The centrality of sex to human relationships

ADULTERY INVOLVES INTENSE FOCUS

Having established that monogamy runs completely against the grain of human nature, we may now understand the centrality of sex in marriage and the need for couples to have the most passionate intimate lives possible (a) if they are to remain together at all, and (b) if they are to remain faithful to each other. The idea of using adultery to rekindle passion in marriage is only important if you truly understand how important a good sex life is to marriage.

But nowadays, people don't like hearing this. Most people today feel that sex is not one of the loftier pursuits of man, and is even somewhat degrading. When I tell my students at Oxford that once upon a time people actually married because it was the only way they could have sex, they look at me in horror and astonishment. A student stood up during a lecture I gave and said, 'Of all the superficial, silly things I have ever heard, to tell us we should marry for sex. My God!' I rose and I thumped my hand on the desk and shouted (for effect), 'Superficial and silly? That's what sex is for you? Of course that's what it has become. The Jewish religion sees sex as the ultimate form of *knowledge* and union. In the Bible and the Hebrew language, there isn't even a word for "sex". The word for "sex" is "knowing", as in "And Adam *came to know* his wife, Eve." '

The problem is that today sex is not a form of knowledge; it has become far too casual. You can have sex with a woman, see her on the street the next day, smile and keep on walking. But sex is the most intense experience we have in life, and should be the thing that we all look forward to most. It has the power to make everything else appear insignificant. If a husband and wife have a good sex life, then the fact that dinner isn't ready on time just doesn't matter so much.

Marriage is different from friendship

Sex is certainly not the only important thing in marriage. But it is what changes a friendship into a marriage. You are not husband and wife when you share a home or apartment. Nor are you husband and wife when you merely share a bedroom. You are specifically husband and wife when you share *the same bed* and enjoy intimate moments of loving.

A major trend in the United States is the celibate marriage. This is built on the idea that no marriage can really preserve its passion and that makes people hung up on the sexual problems in their relationships. So, who needs sex in marriage at all? Just focus on the really important things, like going to art galleries together, discussing Vivaldi, listening to music, baking bread, talking, communicating.

But that's what you do with everybody else. That's not marriage. Marriage is sharing one bed, and becoming one flesh. It's having children together. Sex is definitely the most important element of a marriage at least in its early and intermediate stages. A couple who still feel very close and loving in old age have engendered that closeness by virtue of the passion they shared earlier in life. Sex is the only thing that can truly keep a man and woman together over a long period of time. And a good sex life in particular is the only thing that will guarantee that they remain faithful to each other. A celibate marriage is like the relationship between best friends: the two people involved may feel closer to each other than to anyone else on earth – but they do not experience the intense passion that only sex brings to a marriage.

Achieving sexual focus

In order to keep their sexual lives together happy, passionate and comfortable, the first thing I would urge couples to do is get rid of the television sets in their bedrooms, immediately. There is no greater obstacle to a couple's concentration on each other than having a television. The men have to compete against the likes of Tom Cruise, Mel Gibson and Arnold Schwarzenegger, the women against Madonna, Michelle Pfeiffer and Margaret Thatcher. That is one problem. But even if it's a Donald Duck cartoon, why should you bring such a terrible distraction into your bedroom where you should be focusing on each other?

Husbands and wives who have nothing else to do in their bedroom have a good time together. They don't just sit and watch television. They enjoy each other's company. Television viewing, just like pornography, separates husband and wife because it means focusing on the images you are looking at and not on each other.

11

Jealousy is essential in every marriage

ADULTERY IS ABOUT INTENSE JEALOUSY

Jealousy is one of the most powerful emotions known to man and is as harmful as it is beneficial. Sexual jealousy on the part of adulterers, their spouses, their lovers or their rivals accounts for one-third of all solved murders in the United States every year! Now imagine what intensity of passion we might have with our spouse if we would turn that jealousy to our advantage and use it as an aphrodisiac in marriage.

Your spouse is more desirable than you think

One of the things that perplexes me most about married people – primarily husbands who begin to lose interest in their wives, sometimes to business pursuits and other times by focusing attention on other women – is just how attractive and desirable their own partners are. In so many cases, not only would other men die for the woman whom the husband is ignoring but also, even more bafflingly, the woman whom the husband now pursues is in no way comparable to his wife; not in beauty and not in personality. What has happened and how can the interest be reclaimed?

This answer is simple. Although the husband's wife

is very desirable and attractive, *he has forgotten it*. This in itself is not so surprising. Just as we can become immune to the beauty of our home, and our fortune at having a good job and living in a rich democratic Western country, we can become indifferent to the people who mean the most to us. As time wears on, we begin to take them for granted.

And then something happens. Because of continued neglect, the man's wife develops a greater desire to socialise with people outside the marriage, and other men also begin to show a greater interest in her. Every man loves catering to a damsel in distress. The husband notices, and now he wishes to reclaim what is his. He begins to regain his interest in his wife, and things start to get exciting again. He understands that he can no longer take her for granted, because she is exhibiting a new independence.

It is not only the fact that he may lose her that causes him to work to re-seduce his wife. Her new-found independence is also exciting and sexy to him. It shows him that she is not as boring as he thought. She is a desirable woman who requires love and attention. Moreover, she has sexual needs that need to be fulfilled, and if her husband won't address them, then she'll find someone who will.

The same applies to the way women view their husbands, of course. I sat once with a famous writer discussing this book. She has also written books on relationships, and we were comparing notes and findings. I spoke to her about my firm belief that passion can be restored into monogamous relationships, and that it is all in the mind. She disagreed vehemently and told me that I was absolutely wrong. Suddenly, she came out with a confession. 'I had an affair,' she said. 'I was married for six years. I loved my husband, but the sex was terrible. I worked in a bookstore at the time, and a man came in one day, and we just hit it off. The two years of my affair with him were the most exciting of my life and actually did much to destroy my marriage. Not because my husband ever found out – he didn't. But because after the excitement I experienced in those two years, and the sensuousness of my lover, my husband simply could not compare. He was a dull bore. I still love him, but I know that now I can never really be excited by him, in comparison to the man I knew.'

But why wasn't it in the mind? Because this was different, she insisted. Her husband simply 'lacked the equipment'. She maintained that he was not nearly as well endowed as her lover. With the best will in the world, and whatever effort he made, he would still be lacking physiologically.

'Did your husband also have an affair?' I asked. 'After all, if you were running around with someone else, he must have noticed your loss of interest in him. Did he do anything about it?' 'No,' she answered. 'He's simply not the type. He probably didn't notice anything anyway, because he's not that interested in sex.'

Just two weeks later she called me, shaken to the core. She had discovered that her husband had indeed been carrying on an affair over the last year. She had been tipped off by his mistress's husband, and had driven to the woman's place of work and confronted her. Her husband's mistress admitted to the affair, and told her at length how she did not desire to be a homebreaker, and hoped that the wife would forgive her. But what could she do? She found the woman's husband the sexiest, most passionate man alive and did not feel that she could give him up. To her he was irresistible.

In the end, her husband decided to return to his wife, and their marriage continues till today, albeit with outstanding problems still seeking resolution. But the point had been proven. So much for lacking the right equipment. So much for being a bore. And so much for not being the kind of man who would ever be interested in an affair. Perhaps if she had recognised all these things about her husband sooner, she might have prevented both her own affair and his.

Jealousy rekindles passion

Did you ever have the experience of rummaging through old clothes you wish to donate to charity and chancing upon an old outfit which has lost its appeal? A close friend who is helping you notices the outfit and says that it is lovely, and that if you are throwing it out anyway, they would like to keep it. Suddenly, you're not so sure that you want to get rid of it any more. Your friend's appreciation for the garment has reawakened your own interest in it as well. But why? Just a moment ago you were adamant that you didn't want it. You were going to throw it out! Ah! But that wasn't because it didn't suit you. You wanted to get rid of it because to you it was *old*, and you had become bored of it. But to your friend it is brand-new. And their excitement about it, coupled with their desire to take it away from you and make it their own, reminds

119

you of just how nice it really is. And suddenly you want it back.

The moment someone else shows an interest in your spouse, you are immediately reminded of how special they are and you want them back. It is *jealousy* that reminds you. Seen through the eyes of your colleague, your 'old' and monotonous spouse suddenly becomes 'new' and exciting again. Alarm bells ring, and something must be done. And you begin to woo your spouse as you did once before . . . until you start taking them for granted again.

Jealousy and love

We must expend every effort to remind ourselves constantly of how precious the people with whom we share our lives really are. Although jealousy is usually destructive, it can also be turned to good. Rather than waiting for the breakdown of a marriage, one must induce a perpetual state of jealousy, which will ensure that each spouse will do everything they can to please and impress their partner – not just in a crisis, but continually.

Now, don't confuse jealousy with unfaithfulness or being untrustworthy. No marriage could last without a husband and wife being fully confident that their spouse will always remain devoted and loyal. If a wife really had to worry about what her husband was doing out late at night, and if a husband had to be concerned about whom his wife was thinking about as they made love, both would be miserable. By jealousy in marriage I do not mean that each spouse *deliberately* seeks to make their partner jealous, or flirts with other people at cocktail parties and the like. Rather, a husband and wife should always be conscious of the interest shown them by other men and women. The fact is that other men will stare at your wife, and other women will look admiringly at your husband. Others appreciate their sexiness and attractiveness, even if you don't. And as you watch and realise that this best friend of yours who is speaking innocently to your wife is very much aware of how lovely she is, a spirit of jealousy should awaken in you as you endeavour to secure her devotion to you.

Jealousy: destructive but necessary

Ancient Jewish teaching has some negative things to say about jealousy. The Talmud advises that a husband should never become too jealous, since this will only lead to anger and bring tension into the marriage. Jealousy can cause one spouse to treat the other insensitively and constantly question their innocence. Being excessively jealous of one's spouse can also lead them to feel claustrophobic, and they might purposely rebel against their imprisonment. Everyone needs their freedom in a relationship.

Nevertheless, the understanding that jealousy might lead a man directly into another woman's arms, or a woman into a man's, has often been misconstrued as meaning that there should never be any jealousy over one's spouse. Books that describe in detail the sexual permissiveness of the 1960s, such as Gay Talese's *Thy Neighbor's Wife*, proclaim that many couples felt that they were enlightened because they could transcend 'petty' jealousies and willingly give over their spouses to other sexual partners, and even watch. The celebrated philosopher Bertrand Russell had an arrangement with his wife whereby each could have any lover they wished and they would even tell each other about it afterwards. Justifying this arrangement, he wrote, 'A man or woman who has been thwarted sexually is apt to be full of envy; this generally takes the form of moral condemnation of the more fortunate.' How foolish! A lack of jealousy betrays a lack of love. We all seek to protect the things we love, and desire that they always remain attached to us. If we love someone, we seek to protect and possess.

This is why open marriages, whereby husbands and wives seek to transcend jealousy, always lead to heartache and misery. Russell did not believe in jealousy. However, when his wife Dora had a child by another man, he left her, later commenting, 'My capacity for forgiveness, and what might be called Christian love, was not equal to the demands I was making on it . . . I was blinded by theory.' Their daughter Kathleen Tait pithily remarked about her parents' strange marriage, 'Calling jealousy deplorable had not freed them from it . . . both found it hard to admit that the ideal had been destroyed by the old-fashioned evils of jealousy and infidelity.'

In the book of Proverbs, King Solomon declares that 'one thing opposite the other did God create'. This encapsulates a very profound Jewish thought, namely that everything in life has both a good, positive dimension and an evil, negative dimension. Good things can be used for evil purposes, and bad things for good purposes. In the Bible God is constantly referred to as being a jealous God, as in 'your God is a jealous God'. This certainly suggests a positive aspect of jealousy.

The marriage relationship between a man and woman is meant to reflect the relationship that exists between God and man in general, and God and the Jewish people in particular. The fact that God is jealous of the Jewish people, and cannot tolerate their worshipping foreign gods and idols, is proof that he loves them.

By being constantly mindful of our spouse's *potential* to be adulterous, and of their attraction and attractiveness to others, we can utilise jealousy to enhance our efforts to be engaged in wooing and winning their affections at all times. In this way we can further make our marriages into an illicit affair. Every man or woman involved in an adulterous affair lives in an intense state of jealousy since they cannot dominate their lover completely, and they know that their lover has another life of which they are not a part. We must work to induce this same state of jealousy in marriage.

12

Trust in marriage

ADULTERY IS ABOUT TRUST

'In the man, jealous aggression tends to concentrate on the partner. The woman more frequently extends the aggression to the rival and third parties!'

Daniel Lagache, *La Jalousie Amoureuse* (1947)

'The possibility of adultery', as I have called it throughout this book, is a double-edged sword, and using it to remind ourselves that our spouses are sexual beings, and thus to recapture the passion and excitement in our marriages, traps us in a powerful and very hurtful Catch-22. On the one hand, we need jealousy and the recognition of the sexual attractiveness of our spouses in order to preserve and renew our relationships since we are reminded of the need to win their attention every day of the year. On the other hand, this process leads to hurt and pain as we re-examine our own sexual appeal, and wonder what it is that our spouses see in others that we may not possess, whether we are their equals, and, finally, how serious and deeply felt is their attraction to someone else.

Dealing with jealousy

The Oxford University L'Chaim Society of which I am director is supported entirely by private donations. Some of its supporters are prominent international businessmen, with hundreds of employees working for them. I was once privy to an argument between two of my closest married friends over the issue of hiring a secretary. When the husband's principal assistant of ten years got married to an American and moved to the States, he was very sad to lose her. His wife also worked in the business, in charge of their publicity and public relations department. Together they scoured all the employment agencies in search of a suitable replacement. One day, a woman's CV that seemed too good to be true came through the fax machine. In subsequent interviews with Henry, she proved to be the perfect candidate whom they had thought they would never find. He wanted to hire her instantly.

But his wife objected, and told him that in no circumstances would she allow him to hire her. The woman was young, very attractive, and dressed highly seductively. In her first interview she even came with one of the middle buttons in her blouse open, exposing her bra. The wife insisted that she knew that type of woman, and that she had left her button undone intentionally. The man and his wife had a huge fight over the matter. She called me in tears and in mid-conversation he grabbed the telephone and told me that he is a generous husband and father, allowing for his wife's extravagant tastes. 'But someone's got to pay all these bills, Shmuley, and I need an efficient assistant. This woman is perfect, and I am not prepared to give her up just because of my wife's insane jealousies.' He was adamant. 'Let my wife go and see a psychiatrist. I am not giving up this secretary.'

Of all the irrational elements to be found within the behaviour of a spouse, jealousy is the most trouble-some. Many husbands and wives are utterly unable to deal with their spouse's jealousy, and treat it as some-thing that betrays a deep character flaw in their spouse, something that they must 'work at, or it will destroy our marriage'. They rarely consider the possibility that perhaps, regardless of whether or not their spouse is justified in insisting that they not speak to 'so and so', maybe they should abstain, just to preserve the peace of the marriage and keep their spouse happy. No, this jealousy has got to change and their husband/wife will just have to accept it.

The flaw in this thinking is that it will *not* change. The fact is that the confident and flirtatious way that some men and women speak to our spouse, and the way in which our spouse responds to them, just rubs us up the wrong way, and it always will. Worse still, the attitude that 'my spouse is being irrational and therefore I will not accommodate them' is predicated on the idea that we are obliged to conform to the desires of our spouse only if they appear to us to make sense.

Ask yourself: why is it that your spouse feels so insecure? Have you hurt them significantly in the past? Have you had an affair? And if you haven't, maybe you have shown too much attention to someone in the past and given your spouse good cause to be jealous. Or maybe you simply haven't shown your own spouse *enough* attention. Maybe they feel neglected and un-loved. Maybe they feel that *to you* they are no longer attractive, so that any close association you have with a member of the opposite sex makes them feel insecure. Something, however subtle, is causing your spouse to be uncontrollably jealous.

I firmly advocate that the jealousies of one's spouse must be accommodated, tied as they are to their essential masculinity and femininity. Your husband is jealous of the close association you have with your driving instructor because your husband is a man. Don't ask him why. That's the way men are. If you think he's being irrational, then discuss it with him. Try and make him see your point of view. But if he won't, then find a different instructor. Your husband, along with his seemingly irrational desires, should come first.

Similarly, as I told my friend in the above situation, your wife's jealousy obviously results from her being your wife. That's the way some women are. She wants you to herself and feels insecure when you will be spending more time in your office with a woman who she feels does not respect your marital commitments than you will be spending at home with her. To be sure, your business is important. But your wife is *more* important. Accommodate her on this request; don't tell her to stifle her essential femininity and the love, and hence jealousy, that she feels towards her husband.

The bond of trust

The healthiest resolution to the problem of jealousy is that of trust. So long as we know, not just believe, but *know*, in the core of our being, that our spouse loves us and will always remain loyal and faithful, then we can remain fully aware of the sexual attraction they pose to others outside the marriage, and how they themselves are naturally attracted to others, without fearing that the marriage will be compromised. It is imperative, therefore, not to allow any form of adultery to gain a foothold. I realise this is easier said than done, but it is vital if we are to instil faith and trust in our marriages, and not become insanely jealous, devouring each other in the process. With trust we gain the best of both worlds: the constantly reinvigorating knowledge that the people we are married to are wonderfully attractive to others, coupled with the flattery that notwithstanding that desirability to others they choose to remain steadfastly loyal to us, in every way.

This is what adulterous lovers enjoy. Amidst the tenuous and unpredictable state of their relationship, they trust each other with their compromising secrets even more than they trust their own spouse. This trust helps them to maintain their passion and devotion. Marriage deserves no less. Put your spouse first in all matters. Make them feel that they never have to worry about your being interested in someone else.

13

Married couples: partners or lovers?

ADULTERY IS ABOUT ATTRACTION

'When we are alone in our bedroom, with our bodies pressed firmly against each other, we rarely talk about the weather or where to go for dinner.'

My friends Jeffrey and Susie Goldstein are happily married. However, he loves football. His wife seems to have no interest in the sport whatsoever. The same thing applies in my own marriage. I used to devote a lot of time to sports but Debbie is not interested. I love video games, Debbie is convinced they are immature. Why would a woman marry a man whose passion is football? Why not marry someone who has the same natural or socialised interests as yourself?

People tell me all the time that they are going out with someone but, although they are in love, they fear they cannot possibly marry the person in question because 'we simply don't have enough in common. We'll run out of things to talk about.' I usually tell such people that if they are correct, and compatibility is all-important, then it is best to marry someone of the same sex. Women have more naturally in common with women, and men with men. Heterosexuality is totally illogical. Why should you love someone who is the opposite?

Attraction versus common interests

Young children tend to gravitate toward members of the same sex since they innately enjoy the same activities together. As they grow older and mature, however, they begin reaching across the divide. Sexual attraction begins to supersede common interests, until in their pubescent years, suddenly their attraction to the opposite sex becomes predominant – permanently.

This is important. One of the fundamental causes of marital breakdown today and the dramatic rise in infidelity is that we have called the wrong shots. We've drawn the wrong conclusions. We have made commonality of interests more important than attraction. *One of the principal reasons for the loss of passion in marriage is that we look upon our spouse first and foremost as a partner sharing our interests in life, rather than as our lover.* This same mistake is not repeated in adultery, where lovers treat each other like sweethearts. We must return to the time in our lives when we saw in our spouse a sexual partner, rather than someone with whom we share so much in common. In marriage you are meant to be lovers, not music or botany lovers.

The truth is that men and women get married because they are attracted to each other, and this attraction is based *not* on shared interests but on sexual magnetism.

Friendship versus sexual attraction

In Judaism, the laws that separate the sexes were designed not to preserve modesty, but to preserve *the distinctions* between men and women. What woman would be flattered to hear that her male friends are not remotely sexually interested in her, or don't even notice that she is female?

There was a student at Oxford who was engaged to be married and had her closest male friend, who was also soon to be married, come to visit her from the United States. They went, with her fiancé's permission, on a trip to a different city. They shared a hotel room, although they had separate beds. I said to both of them, 'The two of you are engaged. Why did you allow such a stupid thing?' She replied, 'My fiancé trusts me and this man is my closest friend. We weren't going to do anything.' But is this flattering? Do you want to know that your friend does not find you desirable? Is it good that in our society, men and women have become immune to each other's sexuality?

One of our L'Chaim Society committee members was the kind of girl whom all of the men would come to talk to about their emotional problems. She was every guy's best friend, but never anyone's girlfriend. She walked into my office one day and closed the door, saying she wanted to tell me about something she was upset about. I told her to open the door, for it is a Jewish law that a man and woman who are not married cannot be secluded together in a room. 'I'm a married man and you're a single woman,' said, 'so we can't be in a room with the door closed.' She started to cry. I asked her what the matter was. It is a law, I told her, I am not trying to offend you. She said, 'I'm not crying because you offended me, but because that is the most beautiful thing that anyone has ever said to me. You are the first person who has ever treated me like a woman.' Most men who had looked upon her had made her feel as if they were looking at another man instead of a woman.

There is nothing flattering about pretending that your friends of the opposite sex are not attractive, however good friends they are. There are reasons for the centrality of modest dress in the Jewish religion, specifically women wearing feminine garb as opposed to clothing indistinguishable from a man's. You are not supposed to be the same. It doesn't mean women should be subordinate to men, but that they should retain their essential differences. I believe that husbands should not become best friends with other women, nor wives with other men, not only because it may be improper, but because it is still sending the wrong signals even if nothing happens. It means that you are not seeing other people as women and men. Remember, marriage itself thrives on the differences, and hence the attraction, between men and women.

When husbands and wives are having difficulties in their marriages, and they are not sexually interested in one another, they often don't address the problem directly. They will go to a cinema, or a concert together. Is that why you got married, because you both love music? There is no passion in your marriage because you haven't seen enough of Tom Cruise lately? Forget the damned film. Do something about your love-life. Don't go shopping together. Do as two lovers would. Go to bed. If a husband and wife devoted just half as much time to their sexual encounters as they do to their social calendars, they would have the greatest marriage on earth.

Of course, commonality of interests is important. But the differences that separate men and women are essential. You will never be infatuated or in love with someone because you are compatible. That's all rubbish. You might do business with them, you might go on trips with them. But you won't share their bed every single night because of that. You will do so because of attraction – physical, spiritual and emotional – and attraction only.

14

Nourishing a marriage

ADULTERY BOOSTS THE EGO; AS SUCH, IT IS AN
ACT OF RE-CREATION

The ultimate definition of love, I believe, is a relationship in which two people transform each other's existence into something more beautiful through their affection for each other. When you love someone, their wishes become your wishes, their delights become your delights, their pleasures become your pleasures. Anything else is not love but selfishness. Love gives us the ability to put ourselves second to someone else, thereby defying our essential human nature to be selfish.

If you live on this planet 90 years, but no one ever takes notice of you, it is as if you do not exist. And neither do you feel as if you are ever really alive. The ultimate negation of another person's existence is to ignore them. And the ultimate affirmation of their existence is to love and take notice of them.

This is the enormous power of love. Through loving someone intensely we can call forth their existence from nothingness, playing the role of creator, bringing them to life. And by cheating on them and in effect ignoring them, we play the role of a creator who takes life. Whereas love enhances and uplifts our spouse's existence, adultery degrades and destroys it.

The problem with marriage

Upon assuming my responsibilities in Oxford as Rabbi at the age of 21, I was convinced that the greatest challenge in marriage was the simple difficulty of two people, each accustomed to their own way of life, now sharing their life with another person, and somehow accommodating each other's idiosyncrasies. But as time developed, I began to understand that the real problem was sexual. Why was it, after all, that when people dated before marriage they were far more willing to bend and give in to each other, just in order to impress each other? And why was it so much more difficult after marriage? The answer of course is that once people are married, they begin to take each other for granted, and no longer make so much effort to win the love and sexual favours that they once wished to discover.

Why on earth is it that a husband or wife would rather argue over dinner not being ready, and refuse to apologise after an outburst, thereby ending up spending the night in separate bedrooms, instead of falling into each other's embrace and experiencing an evening of love and bliss? The only explanation can be that sometimes we just do not value that embrace and that act of love enough. If we desired sex with our spouse badly enough, we would do anything to get it – just as adulterous lovers do. Far from being our enemy, sex is our friend, and must be used to our advantage. The same cause for adultery, namely a desire for passion and sex, can also be used as the main pretext for a husband and wife to begin to treat each other, once again, with love, caring and honesty.

The essential elements of a relationship

There are four recognitions essential to every thriving relationship. First, that the person we are married to is not just a spouse or a person, but a *sexual being*. Secondly, that they have sexual needs and crave to be desired. Thirdly, that they are sexually attractive to other people who will risk all to have an affair with them. And finally, bringing all these things together, that they are not so much under our spell and control as we once thought. We must strive hard to retain their attention and affection, and if we do not, since they are sexual beings, we will lose them.

Fulfilling every need

Any husband or wife who is a decent person and loves the person they are married to is willing, as far as they are able, to fulfil each and every desire of their spouse. However, there is one important proviso to this willingness: the request has to make sense. When it doesn't, the trouble starts. For example, a wife tells her husband how much she loves flowers and asks him, if he plans to buy her anything, to please put flowers at the top of his list. He replies that flowers die quickly. 'I can't understand why you're insisting on me buying things with such a short life span; they're a waste of money!' He agrees to buy her silk clothing and sparkling jewellery instead. She grows angry and insists that he cannot love her unless he does what she has asked. He then demands that at the very least she should explain herself to him, but she cannot. Where is the woman who can truly explain why women love flowers? Yet he insists that he cannot appreciate or respond to her request unless she can rationalise it for him. In the meantime, he continues to buy her even more expensive gifts, and she continues to be miserable.

This husband is making a twofold mistake. The first part is in the context of his being in a relationship. Being in a relationship means being responsive to the needs of your partner. If you choose to fulfil only those desires of your partner that make sense to you, then your relationship is *de facto* a relationship with yourself. There is no room for a partner to exist as himself or herself in such a relationship, since only when they comply with what *you* think is rational are they taken seriously. Being in a relationship means trying your best to please the person you say you love. It doesn't mean doing what you *think* will please them, amidst their incessant protestations. In a relationship you first listen, and then you give.

The woman *in your wife; the* man *in your husband*

The second mistake that the husband makes is far more significant. By saying that he will do whatever she wants as long as she explains herself, he is insisting that he be connected only to her intellectual, rational side. Her deeper, truer self remains a mystery to him, a part of her with which he has no association. *This man is not married to all of his wife.* In fact, he is not joined to the part of her that is most attractive: her womanhood.

There is an essential femininity in his wife which, since he is male, he will never understand. There is nothing she can possibly do that can convey to him her intrinsic desire for flowers. It completely transcends logic, *but this does not invalidate its importance*. On the contrary, it is the very differences between male and female that sustain their attraction.

By telling his wife that she doesn't know what she wants, or insisting that her demands are foolish or don't make sense, this husband refuses to acknowledge her independence as a human being. But when he actually fulfils her every wish, whether or not he understands it, he ensures that he is connected with her innermost self. Only now is he married to his wife in her entirety, which also encompasses the part of her that is essentially different from him, that is, the *woman* in his wife.

Likewise, if a woman denies her husband's right to be different, by refusing accommodate his (what appear to her to be) irrational desires, she is forgetting that her husband is not just a breadwinner and father – he is the *man* she married, and she must cherish him or lose him.

Show your spouse extravagant love. Show them overwhelming interest, to constantly boost their confidence. Show them through tangible action that they have nothing to fear from people outside the marriage. Show your spouse how attracted you are *to them*, how beautiful or handsome you find them. Prove to them that you remain fully focused on your spouse. Even if you are forced *to go to an extreme* for a while in terms of behaving unnaturally and avoiding conversation with other men or women, do it. Your spouse will feel loved and special and confident and trustful in your relationship.

Marriage is a hungry animal, and needs to be fed constantly.

15

Restoring passion in marriage

ADULTERY IS ABOUT PASSION, EXCITEMENT, AND NEWNESS

Can passion *really* be maintained within a mono-gamous relationship, or will my writing this book prove an exercise in futility?

All too many people think that the jury is already in with a definite settlement. While marriage can provide support and security, it cannot maintain its excitement. Every week in Oxford I hold a debate on some import-ant social or religious issue, in front of a student audience. When I once made the case for marriage, the audience conceded that my arguments had been con-vincing, and one student stood up and said, 'Yeah, I guess it is worthwhile to sacrifice passion for the sake of stability.' Everyone else agreed. And that shocked me. *Sacrifice what for what?* What was he on about? Why is there an assumption that having many sexual partners is more passionate and more exciting than having a single sexual partner with whom one is really and truly in love?

This is one of the greatest fallacies and must be refuted. Rediscovering passion in sexual relations in-volves not a change in partner but a change in attitude. We equate passion with newness, and finding a new partner will almost certainly result in very passionate sex. But it is a shortcut that has no permanence. For how long can a new partner remain new? For a long-term solution to the problem of 'monotony through familiarity', we must search for something new in our partner, on a regular basis.

The dullness of the marriage bed

Is having sex with the same partner over a long time a preordained ticket to erotic boredom? Here are comments from three married men:

'... I've been married 16 years now and been completely faithful to my wife. I'd have to say, in all candour, that our sexual relationship now is much better than it was when we were first married. To me, the trick has been to be creative about our sex lives – not with whips and chains, or gymnastic positions – but with keeping away from routines; and staying attuned to each other's needs. For instance, we've learned to spend a lot of time giving each other sensual massages as part of our foreplay. It's an almost incredible, tantalising delight...'

Less positively, a 44-year-old man says, 'Let's face it, my wife isn't as attractive as she once was, she's let her body go to pot, and her idea of good sex is [coitus] twice a week. It's like she's doing me a favour. Is it any wonder I say our sex life is boring?... So I go to a classy hooker once a month as my way of getting even...'

A 49-year-old man: 'Although I've been happily married for 27 years, I've certainly noticed a definite deterioration in our sex life. We get along really well, we do more together now than we ever did, but sex is the one area in our lives where we seem in such a rut. I'm not sure who's to blame for it, since I think we're both involved, but I guess we've both given up too easily, accepting a lousy sex life as a given. I'm not proud to admit it, but the way I've coped with this for years is by having occasional affairs. At least that way I feel like I can still turn someone on.'

The last two accounts surely seem damaging for they portray an all too common scenario. But is it inevitable? The answer is, of course not. Only lazy and uncreative people will lose passion in their marriage and take the easy way out by finding excitement with someone else, until they get bored with this partner too.

Creativity and romance

Even the most secular sex therapists agree that capitulating to monotony in marriage is ridiculous and avoids the central issue. Their advice is not to vary your partner, but to vary your routine. 'To avoid too much "sameness" in sex, don't always try to get amorous at the same time of day, change the scenery on occasion (for instance try sex some place other than your bedroom, whether it means checking into a hotel for a night or sending the kids to sleep at friends' homes so you can make love in front of the living-room fireplace), and vary the action.'

Other practical suggestions include introducing new options into your sexual interactions, such as experimenting with sensual massage, and new types of sexual activity that you have never tried before, experimenting with different positions and foreplay, changing venues, and so on. But having read tens of books on similar subjects in preparation for writing this one, I can tell you that often this advice can itself suffocate creativity and stultify the emotions. My own personal immediate advice is this: do unto your wife whatever you would do if you wished to seduce your secretary, business assistant or airline stewardess. Do unto your husband what you would do to that sexy fellow lawyer if you wanted him to think you a sex goddess. Surely you have ideas as to how you would win them over to you, and how you would pleasure them. Let your own sexual creativity run riot. Make your marriage into an illicit affair. Your wife's opinion of your sexual virility is no less important than the woman next door's.

Sexuality is not an entity on its own, but is a natural outcome of a loving and romantic relationship. So the best way of enhancing one's sexual life is not to try to implement new sexual positions and techniques, but to bring greater romance into everyday life. Preserving romance is an ongoing challenge, which bids us focus on those small, non-sexual interactions of affection, which sadly have become all too rare. How many people today write love letters to their spouse? And how many buy flowers for absolutely no reason other than as a sign of affection for the person they love? These gestures aren't just ceremonial. They make a recipient feel loved and appreciated – and can have a direct bearing on the passionate feelings that ensue at bedtime. As Masters and Johnson say, 'It is no surprise that as we fall into non-romantic complacency in our relationships, our sexual interests and passions are apt to dwindle, too.'

If married couples focus purely on their sexual lives outside a romantic framework, if they see nothing in each other but their flesh, they will undoubtedly get bored with each other quickly. If they cannot enjoy conversation, if they do not see the magic of sharing a life with another human being, a creature of limitless depth, then their partner presents nothing new to discover. How many inches of flesh does a person have? Are we really going to be excited by seeing the same thing day after day? But when we peer into each other's soul, if we can be inspired by the infinite beauty of our spouse, inspired enough to write and sing to them about that process of discovery, then how can we possibly become bored? Our marriage then becomes a journey, embarked upon with the express purpose of reaching new heights together.

The erotic effect of desire

In her book about sexual passion *How to Satisfy a Woman Every Time*, author Naura Hayden tells the story of her friend Helen Gurley Brown,

> *a truly beautiful woman, inside and out, and loaded with sex appeal. I'll never forget a couple of years ago when we both were on the plane from New York to Los Angeles. She got up to stretch her legs, and every man on the plane craned his neck to watch her as she reached for her bag, and then headed for the restroom. When I saw her later in Los Angeles at the baggage claim, I told her of all the men eyeing her, and asked her how does she keep so sexy all the time? She gave me a great reply which I could never forget. Helen said she feels so much love from her husband, David, and that it is with her all the time, and it makes her feel sexy all the time. Wow! Now there's a great love affair and a great marriage.*

This is a terrific story, and illustrates an important point. Here is a husband who actually *loves* his wife. He loves her so much, and presumably demonstrates it so readily in thought, speech, and action, that his wife *becomes* physically attractive as a result. Appearances really *aren't* everything. Real love on a deep level is so powerful that it *creates* an aesthetic reality. Not only that, but it creates a situation in which the appeal of aesthetic beauty will never wear off because it is anchored in something far deeper than what is only on the surface. If every single one of us loved our spouse in the manner described above, then they would feel absolutely desirable, and would look, dress and behave accordingly. We would watch them become transformed from an ordinary, bored-looking man or woman into the most conspicuous sex object, radiating appeal.

The point is that any couple who feel that their intimate life together has become monotonous or boring face a choice: either they can admit defeat and accept that their life together will never be passionate, and then either live without passion or find extra-marital sex, or they can fight back. There are wonderful techniques they can employ to change the situation. But the most important factor is a couple's wish to make their marriage work. Don't take harmful short-cuts. Forget about what you could be doing with the man next door. Concentrate on what you're going to do with the man who shares your life.

The key is to master the way in which we look at our spouse and always focus on the sexual possibilities they present. We must see our spouse as an open door sexually, rather than focus on the sexual experiences we have already had with them, which appear to be a closed door. This may indeed be the house that we live in, but the opportunities for construction and decoration are endless.

16

Avoiding temptation

*'People ask me, Do you ever get crushes on
the men you work with? And the truth,
which I usually find ways not to say, is yes,
often, don't you?'*

Peggy Noonan, chief speechwriter to Ronald
Reagan, *What I Saw at the Revolution*

A close friend of mine had just become engaged to a
wonderful girl. She had it all – intelligence, unusual
beauty, the gift of music, sweetness and femininity –
and he felt incredibly lucky. However, it was only a
short time before he began to see her unusual gifts as
something of a curse. For he was not the only one to
whom she appealed. Virtually every man she met found
her desirable as well. In the academic group in which
she worked, she spent many long hours with men who
flirted innocently with her, and others who went as far
as inviting her out and even writing her love letters.
Naturally, she found all this wonderfully flattering, but
her fiancé would have none of it. Angry as hell after
yet another argument with her over the subject and
her refusal to distance herself from men who posed
as courtiers, he came to see me. He demanded that
she remove herself from all the men who were overly
attracted to her. Her defence was that she loved him
with all her heart and would never contemplate doing
anything to hurt him. What possible harm, therefore,

could arise from her getting on with her academic work together with men who worshipped her? So long as she had no interest in them, what could possibly happen?

I have encountered this scenario frequently in my time counselling students and married couples. One partner will begin to attract an admirer or admirers, to the other partner's great jealousy and consternation. The admired spouse will refuse to dissociate themselves from their admirer either because they feel it is innocent, or because they work together, or because they simply find it impossible to extricate themselves from the situation. Often, the admired spouse will be resentful of their spouse's 'misplaced' jealousy, finding it unfairly imprisoning. They will also take great offence at the implication that they might not be faithful.

Beruriah and Rabbi Meir

The Talmud relates the story of Beruriah, the wife of the great luminary Rabbi Meir, one of the most famous Jewish sages of all time. The equally famous Beruriah is one of the most celebrated women in Jewish history, and certainly the best-known woman of the Talmudic era. She was renowned for her devout piety, goodness, and even her scholarship and erudition, which were unusual for a woman in that period. Ironically, however, she met a humiliating and tragic end. Here is her story as the Talmud relates it:

> *Rabbi Meir fled to Bavel. Some say it was a result of the episode involving his wife Beruriah. Once, she ridiculed the Sages' statement that women*

are suggestible. *Rabbi Meir said to her, 'By your life, someday you will acknowledge the truth of their words.' Rabbi Meir appointed one of his students to try to seduce her. It took a long time, but he was very persistent, and she finally agreed. When she found out that it was all a charade orchestrated by Rabbi Meir she strangled herself. Not expecting such a turn of events, Rabbi Meir fled to Bavel out of shame and grief.*

The point of the story is not to demonstrate the 'suggestibility' of women, nor the propensity of even the strongest-willed or most righteous women to be seduced. Rather, the story illustrates the suggestibility of *all humans*, and how none of us is immune to flattery, love and attention. And far from being a weakness, this is one of the most sublime human virtues.

In fact, the Talmud does not spare even the reputation of Rabbi Meir himself, of whom we are told the following story:

Rabbi Meir used to ridicule people who sinned, because he felt that it was not that difficult to overcome the evil inclination. One day Satan, who is the source of the evil inclination, appeared to Rabbi Meir in the guise of a beautiful woman standing on the other side of a river. There were no boats available for crossing the river, only a rope bridge. Rabbi Meir grabbed onto the rope and started making his way across the river. When Rabbi Meir had gone halfway across the river his evil inclination released him from its grip.

Satan said to Rabbi Meir, 'Were it not

proclaimed in the heavens to take heed of Rabbi Meir and his Torah, I would have reduced you to two small heaps of remains.'

In relating the efforts of even the great Rabbi Meir to reach the beautiful but forbidden woman, the Talmud seeks to emphasise not his weakness, but his *humanity*. There is nothing wrong with being attracted to other people and responding to their affections. Indeed, if we did not react this way, we wouldn't be soft or vulnerable enough to exist within a loving relationship. Think about it. Can you honesty say that, despite the jealousy you feel when you see your spouse sexually interested in another, you would prefer it if they were immune to the rest of the world sexually? Would you prefer a dispassionate partner in life, and someone who is completely unattractive to others? As far as married people are concerned, the only thing wrong with reciprocating a stranger's affections is that it contradicts the marriage and encroaches on the core of emotions that should be reserved exclusively for one's spouse.

Sex should be out of control

How, then, can we remain loyal in thought, speech and action to the one we love? How can two opposites coexist? On the one hand, repressing our sexuality is unhealthy, and acknowledging our attraction and attractiveness to others is positive and leads to excitement in marriage. But on the other, actually committing adultery destroys in one fell swoop everything in marriage that we had hoped to achieve!

The answer is never to put ourselves into the kind of

situation where we will be forced to fight our natural, healthy emotions; never to find ourselves in an intimate environment with a member of the opposite sex who is not our spouse, in which a natural attraction can begin to develop, which we really don't desire, and which we will be forced to resist. Contrary to popular thinking, you're no hero if you can control your sexual urge. Sexual instinct is not meant to be controlled. Really exciting sex means *losing* control. Jewish laws vigorously maintain that a man and a woman who are not married should not be secluded together, and should not allow themselves to be put into situations in which they will have to resist. Having to resist one's sexual urge turns sex into something that demands control, thus diminishing the real passion of sex which occurs only when one's senses, emotions and libido are on auto-pilot.

Of course, compromising situations will arise now and then even if one steadfastly tries to avoid them, and I am not suggesting that we should have no control over our sexual selves, and succumb to every passion the moment it arises. Make no mistake. I am not writing a book in favour of adultery. Indeed, all sexual relations must be subject to human will and there must always be a conscious decision involved. (Quite apart from the appalling situation of date rape, or any rape for that matter, even within a marriage there will be times when one partner does not want to have sex when the other does, and the one who does must restrain themselves. Jewish law is adamant that there can be no sex in marriage unless it is undertaken willingly, even joyfully, by both husband and wife.) But at the very least one must seek to avoid getting oneself entangled in a situation where one will be forced to suppress one's sexuality. Repression is not healthy.

Keep your distance

Should men and women then be segregated? Should we seek to limit the natural and innocent interaction between men and women because they might allow it to develop into a full-blown affair?

Of course not. The secret, once again, is modesty. First, we must dress modestly. A man or woman who dresses provocatively is making a statement that they desire to be noticed. And while it is fine to be noticed, it is a different statement when we want to be noticed first and foremost for our sexuality.

Secondly, and more importantly, we must speak and behave modestly. This means refraining from overt sexual discussions with colleagues. It also means not speaking too personally about our intimate lives with men and women to whom we are not married. Unless we are totally deadened sexually, *speaking about sex gets us excited about sex*. By encouraging or initiating discussion about our sex lives, we are unwittingly, and perhaps innocently, issuing an invitation to outsiders to join in our personal life. We are also telling them that we want them to be exposed to our intimate selves, and that we are somewhat dependent on them in areas that should be reserved exclusively for our spouses. Marriage is only sacred if it is intimate and personal. Refrain from making it a public affair. Ask any husband or wife how they would feel if they discovered that their spouse was divulging the most intimate details of their personal lives to friends at the office. They would be mortified, and that's the way it should be. It is not only the sex in a marriage that is private.

But modest behaviour also means not staring at a colleague with the kind of look that will tell them you are definitely interested in them and find them stimulating. Even if you feel it, don't show it. It means not excessively complimenting your employee or co-worker to the point where they must question why they have suddenly become your obsession. It also means being careful about going for drinks together in isolation or even with other co-workers, enjoying another man or woman's company in a non-working environment, for this affords the opportunity to enjoy the other person not just as a colleague but as a man or a woman. Remember: men and women are not like Teflon, they are like Velcro. They are naturally drawn to one another and naturally stick. Therefore, keep some distance.

Modesty in thought

Of course, the two premises above are predicated on the most important premise of all: thinking modestly. If we fantasise about our colleagues and see them in a sexual light, or if we look at them sexually, it is inevitable that, first, we will give ourselves away and they will know exactly what we are thinking and, second, we will either begin to act upon this longing or damage ourselves through repression. Modesty of thought is the most important guarantee that we will remain steadfastly loyal to our spouse. It also means that we won't be tempted to think about someone else when we are in bed with our husband or wife. It is not sufficient merely to refrain from having sexual affairs; we must not fantasise about them either. If you feel you absolutely must fantasise in order to generate personal excitement when you are in bed with your spouse, then *fantasise about your spouse* in an erotic situation.

Our spouse is a man or a woman; everyone else is a human

The manner in which we perceive the men and women to whom we are married should be first and foremost sexual. But people to whom we are not married should be first and foremost *people* to us, even though we are not immune to their sexuality and we realise that they are also either male or female. If a man has a female co-worker, he may respect her intelligence and her efficiency, but he should not dwell on her charm as a woman. And although they may have a close working relationship and enjoy each other's company immensely, they must still keep their distance. A husband should not focus on his co-worker's legs or bust, but on her personality and humanity. He must see her in the generic. Not female, but human.

Part of keeping one's distance is ensuring that all forms of physical contact are kept to a minimum. Once we become aware of someone as an attractive man or woman, rather than purely as a person, the danger light is on. As one 33-year-old secretary in New England who had an affair with a co-worker put it, it all started when 'He bent over in front of me to fix my typewriter, and I couldn't resist his body.'

Another woman says, 'I never intended to have an

affair. My lover is my former college professor who shares my love of literature. We started this relationship very innocently, by having lunch after class and discussing the class. I found him to be caring, sensitive, understanding, and very sexy.' It was specifically the transition from having a professional relationship and having discussions about literature, to noticing his caring and sensitivity as a man, that led to the affair.

Can you have close friends of the opposite sex?

A close friend of mine married late in life. Although he loved his wife dearly, he was already settled in his course in life, and had many friends, a number of whom his wife objected to. One such friend was a woman his own age, whom he had known for many years. About six months after their marriage, the husband insisted that he was going to Cannes, on the French Riviera, with this woman friend. His wife was flabbergasted and I was called in. She simply could not believe that her husband was planning to go away for the weekend with a female friend. But he, for his part, couldn't understand what all the fuss was about. 'Look, Shmuley,' he told me, 'I have known this girl for ten years. We are close friends and the friendship has always been platonic. I can control myself. I just don't want the friendship to collapse, so I'm going to spend some quality time with her. And we're not going to stay in the same room together.'

I told him, 'Andy, this is wrong. And not because I believe that something will happen. I believe you when you say that nothing will. It's wrong because when a man and a woman go away together, alone, for a weekend, something *should* happen. The very fact that one is male and one is female, and they are secluded, should be exciting and stimulating. Are you proud of the fact that you have deadened yourself sexually to women, or even this one woman? And how about your friend? What if she was in this room and heard you saying you did not find her attractive, were not turned on by her, and so there was nothing to worry about? Would she be happy, or would she feel offended? Can she possibly be flattered when you tell her, "I can go away with you for a weekend and nothing will happen because I am completely oblivious to the woman in you, and for me it is just like going away for a weekend with a man?" That's why it is wrong. Because you are not supposed to put yourself into situations in which the only way out, and the only way in which you can preserve your fidelity to your wife, is by turning yourself off sexually.'

About two months later I was delivering a series of lectures to 18-year-old high school students. I told them this story, and my friend's arguments, and asked them their opinion. I was startled to discover that 38 of the group of 40 said that there was nothing wrong with his going away for the weekend with this woman. Their reasoning was that there is nothing wrong with men and women being good friends. In fact, they told me, they applauded his maturity and sexual liberation. His action showed he respected women and didn't just see them as sexual objects.

'Give me a break,' I told them. 'It is one thing to say that a woman does not want to be treated *exclusively* as a sex object. It is quite another thing to say that women are actually happy when their sexuality and their intrinsic femininity, their very womanhood, is completely overlooked. That's rubbish. Far from being a compliment, telling someone that they are not attractive as a man or a woman is *the* biggest insult.' Conversely, the fact that we are all potentially capable of committing adultery, because we are all attractive, sensual creatures, is a compliment to us. But it also means that we must always be on our guard against things getting out of hand.

Real marriage means being devoted in thought, speech and action to one's spouse, at all times and in all circumstances. Most of all, it means being devoted even in the subtle nuances of love, and in the predicaments in which one finds oneself. Fidelity in marriage is expressed not only by not going to bed with someone else, but also by not sharing any of those special secluded moments, which are so important to a marriage, with someone else. At all times, what a husband or wife should consider in their interactions with members of the opposite sex is this: if their spouse were watching them at this moment, would they be happy or angry? Would they feel pride, or would they feel humiliation? Would their love increase or diminish? And, most of all, would they object?

A married friend of mine was at the beach when an attractive young woman whom he didn't know walked up to him and asked if he wouldn't mind administering suntan lotion on her back, shoulders and legs. 'Sure,' he said, and happily complied.

'How could you?' I asked him when he told me later.

'Come on, Shmuley,' he said. 'Stop being such a religious prude.'

'Well,' I said, 'if there really is nothing wrong with

what you did, then I assume you wouldn't mind my telling your wife about this insignificant little episode.'

And at this he balked, and admitted that had his wife been there with him, he wouldn't have done it. So why did he? 'If I'd said no, I would have offended her. Her intentions were completely innocent.'

'Maybe,' I said, 'but why don't you think of your wife's feelings before this stranger of a woman? It was not this woman at the beach to whom you undertook real obligations, but the woman who is sitting and waiting for you at home.'

Real love and respect in marriage mean always behaving as though your spouse is present. It is where people are courageous enough to employ this rule at all times that happy marriages are found.

17

The pain of adultery

*'When Harold told me he was leaving home
to move in with a woman he'd met at his
office, I just collapsed. I simply could not
believe it ... Whenever I did have to go out
to get some necessity or other, I was so paranoid I thought everybody was staring at me,
thinking "Poor, pathetic thing; no wonder
her husband dumped her." '*

Diane Baroni and Betty Kelly, *How to Get Him
Back from the Other Woman*

On a speaking tour of North America I asked a group
of Jewish women to think how they would feel if they
discovered that their husband was having or had had
an affair. Understandably, most said that they would
be extremely hurt, and many went as far as to state
that their whole world would collapse. The men in the
audience were less vocal on the subject, but basically
expressed the same sentiment. Because I wanted them
to explore the underlying meaning of marriage, I asked
the women exactly why they would be hurt. The
answer seems obvious, but it leads to a better understanding of what marriage is all about. The consensus
was that an affair would mean that their husband loved
or was infatuated with somebody else, and that was
the ultimate form of rejection. To have your husband
commit adultery with someone, they said, was to be

discarded like so much useless waste.

Fair enough. But what if it wasn't a long-standing affair, just a one-night stand while he was on a business trip? He obviously did not love the woman involved. He did it merely because he felt the urge, knowing full well that he loved his wife, and this was just a form of adventurism or sexual release, perhaps to cure the pangs of loneliness, or perhaps a brief quest for danger and excitement. In short, the husband thought it was no big deal. Would they still be hurt?

They said yes, most definitely. But I wanted to know why. I eliminated the elements that might distract us from the real reason we find infidelity unacceptable: 'Why would you be upset? He did not love her, so you can't feel rejected. Suppose he even says that while the whole thing was going on, he was thinking about his wife! And it just happened to be that you, his wife, were not around, so what was he to do? And you also can't say that it means that he is attracted to other women and that's painful. First of all, because every spouse is somewhat attracted to people outside their marriage, although of course they may not do anything about it. Secondly, perhaps you, the wife, are far more attractive. What then? He only committed a sexual act with this other woman because his wife was not around and, for all intents and purposes, it appears that he had no other motive and he is telling the truth. So why be upset at all?' Here suddenly the audience was at a loss as to how respond. It's as if all married people react with revulsion to the thought of their spouse having an affair. But they don't quite know why.

The pain experienced by someone whose spouse has been unfaithful is indescribable and has, tragically, often led to their committing violent murder, suicide, or both. How can we understand such deep pain?

The most profound reason why a wife or husband is upset by infidelity is this: their spouse, someone who belonged to them, was used, even abused, by someone else. As a result, the spouse who was not present was made to feel that they did not exist.

Most people would get upset if someone, even a friend, used their car without permission. Yet if they asked, we might happily allow them to use it, as well as many other possessions. But there are some things that are so personal and so private that we would not allow anyone to use them, such as one's wedding ring or, perhaps, one's bedroom. And how much more so when it comes to one's husband or wife! When they share an intimate experience with someone else, we feel violated, as if someone has used our most intimate object for their personal use but worse, because when we are confronted with infidelity, the feeling of loss and hurt goes right to the core of our being.

The real hurt associated with someone taking your car without your permission has little to do with the fact that the actual car was taken. It may be brought back complete and as good as before. The thief might even have filled the tank up with petrol. So why are you angry? *Because you were not asked!* This belittles you and makes you seem insignificant. The outrage we feel when one of our possessions is used without our permission has little to do with the object itself, and everything to do with ourselves. *It is not the object that has been violated.* We have been violated. We weren't asked. We were treated as if we were not important enough to ask. We were treated as if we did not exist.

A car is only a material possession, but a spouse who cheats on us is making the ultimate statement of our insignificance. We put all of ourselves into our marriage (unlike our car), so that when our spouse betrays us, even if it is just a brief encounter not to be repeated, the hurt is almost impossible to bear, and certainly impossible to forget. With that one action, our spouse, the one who is supposed to make us feel the *most* loved and the *most* significant, the one who is meant to make their universe revolve around us and treat us as if the sun has risen for our sake, has dismissed our existence in its entirety.

Humiliation is a type of murder

No wonder, then, that by far the overriding feeling associated with marital infidelity is *humiliation*, far more than pain, betrayal, or shock. The partner cheated against feels disgraced. In Judaism the biggest crime is to humiliate someone publicly. The Talmud declares that he who humiliates someone publicly loses his share in the world to come, and likens this act to killing. And it is exactly so. In the act of killing, one person decides to negate the existence of another completely. There can be no greater crime, or statement of arrogance, than this. And the same is true of humiliating someone publicly. By humiliating them, you dismiss their existence by destroying their reputation and self-esteem. If you murder someone you incur a capital penalty, thereby losing your place in this world. But if you publicly humiliate someone, you lose your place in the world to come. You die an eternal death. It is a bigger sin to make someone *wish* they were dead than to make them dead.

The worst form of humiliation is adultery. When your husband is unfaithful to you, he is dismissing you completely. He enjoys intimacy with another woman. He acts as if he has no wife, as if he is not married. What wife? He is saying that you don't exist.

A truly fascinating corollary is this: if a man is cheating on his wife and has a mistress, the mistress will be extremely upset to discover that he has a second mistress. Nearly all women who are having an affair with a married man say they would be furious if they discovered that they too were being cheated on. Some go as far as saying, 'I would kill him.' Yet on the other hand, paradoxically, the same women do not give a toss that this same man is having sexual liaisons with his own wife, perhaps even every night. They do not consider this 'cheating'. To them, the wife is nothing. She is not even in competition. It is as though she doesn't even exist. The mistress can be devastatingly jealous of a third woman, but rarely of the wife.

After adultery

It is an inescapable tragedy of adultery that it is the *victim* who is left to feel the culprit, and who is even more hurt and humiliated than a remorseful husband after the event.

Telling your spouse that the adultery was no big deal makes things far worse; it utterly exposes the folly of the typical male defence of infidelity: it was only sex, I didn't love her, it wasn't at all serious. Far from this claim lessening the pain of a man's wife, it just adds insult to injury. The less serious it was, the more it shows that he dismissed the existence of his wife completely. If a husband was tormented and tortured over whether or not he was going to commit adultery, if he felt terrible remorse afterwards, instead of dismissing it as a trivial and passing event, at least then he would be showing that he took his wife into consideration. But when he brushes it off as nothing, he is basically arguing that he *did not reckon at all* with the fact that he was married. It was no big deal. My wife never even came into my deliberations. I acted just as I would have done when I was single, when I didn't have to consider that I might be hurting someone.

If, God forbid, you ever do commit adultery, at the very least don't pretend that it was nothing. While to you it may just have been sex, and you think that you can go back to your wife in good conscience, to your wife it was serious indeed since you made her feel she wasn't your wife at all.

In the *Hite Report*, a woman describes the turmoil her husband's affairs brought into their life:

Over a period of ten years, my husband had been unfaithful. We had gone through several crises, all over one woman, and with the help of marriage counsellors, ministers, relatives, and friends, I had come through. Of a forgiving nature anyway – 'soft' – I wanted the children to have a united family atmosphere to grow up in. I believed my husband would grow out of his 'yearning' for another and accept his responsibilities to our family. He didn't. In the end there was a complete breakdown. He started disappearing literally overnight 'just to sort things out'. I

*was 'only trying to help' and he was 'sorting
things out'. In the end I couldn't take any more.
My husband was always telling me that I didn't
seem to need him as the other woman did. What
he meant was that I managed without him – I
had to – it wasn't that I wanted to.*

This illustrates why, after adultery, the marriage may
never again be the same. The wife may never again be
as loving or caring as she once was. This is not because
she is still angry or vengeful or even because she is
hurt. Rather, it is because she feels that it was her
goodwill itself and her overexertion to be a good wife
that led to her husband's infidelity.

But no more of that. She will make him spend
more time earning her love, rather than seducing other
women. Not out of spite, but because she wants his
emotions firmly fixed on herself rather than someone
else. Quite simply – as is more often than not the case
– in spite of all the hurt and outrage, she still loves
him.

The first marital dispute in the Bible

The first marital dispute in the Bible, recorded in
Genesis 21, is a fascinating story. Sarah and Abraham
wanted children, but Sarah was barren. In an effort to
ensure that Abraham had a son, she gave him her
maidservant Hagar, a former Egyptian princess,
to marry. Abraham therefore had a son through her:
Ishmael, later father of the Arab peoples. But God had
foretold through an angelic guest that Sarah would
also have a child, and his name would be Isaac. Sure

enough, this indeed happened, bringing great joy and happiness into their lives, and especially Sarah's.

However, something then went very wrong. The Bible relates, 'And Sarah saw the son of Hagar the Egyptian, whom she had borne unto Abraham, making sport.' Sarah felt that Ishmael was having an adverse influence on her son Isaac, and so she commanded Abraham to get rid of his son Ishmael. The Bible continues, 'Wherefore she said unto Abraham, "Cast out this bondwoman and her son, for he shall not be heir with my son Issac." ' But Abraham was very unhappy at this; the Bible continues, 'This was very grievous unto the sight of Abraham, on account of his son.'

In this squabble, Sarah seems to put Abraham in a very difficult position; she asks him to cast out Ishmael, who, regardless of the fact that he was born to him of the maidservant, is still his son. Even if he was being an adverse influence, one can only imagine the conflict of loyalties that Abraham must feel. At first glance it would appear that Sarah's request, although perhaps founded on some facts, is unreasonably harsh.

But God suddenly interceded on Sarah's behalf: 'God said unto Abraham, "Let it not be grievous in your eyes because of the lad, and because of the bondwoman; all that Sarah has said unto you, harken unto her voice, for in Isaac shall seed be called unto you." '

Abraham heeded God's advice, and we read that he 'rose early in the morning, took bread and a bottle of water and gave it to Hagar, putting them and the child on her shoulder, and sent her away, and she departed'.

What is particularly interesting about this story is that not only does God deem it necessary to intercede, but furthermore He takes the side of Sarah, the wife.

This seems to be not necessarily because He thinks she is right – her position seems very difficult to sustain, given that she herself gave Hagar to Abraham and told him to have a child with her – but because, regardless of whether she was right or wrong, the essential question was the peace and harmony of the marriage.

For the sake of peace in marriage it is not really important whether an aggrieved party is justly aggrieved or not. So long as they are upset, that is enough. And the vital thing is to end the argument as early as possible. In a marital dispute, harmony is more important than justice.

18

Adultery of the Mind

'But I have more respect for fantasy than that. You are what you dream ... Because sex is all in the head ... What did it matter that "technically" I was faithful to Bennett? I was unfaithful to him at least ten times a week in my thoughts – and at least five of those times I was unfaithful to him when we were making love.'

Erica Jong, *Fear of Flying* (expletives deleted)

Some couples are prepared to undertake the rigorous steps to restore ongoing sexual excitement in their relationships. Others, however, prefer to take short-cuts. What I have found from dozens of conversations is that by far the most common shortcut is fantasising about another man or woman while in bed with one's spouse. This fantasy might involve one's secretary or assistant, business associate, the milkman, or even the glamorous stars of the silver screen. Hey, if you can't actually take the person of your dreams to bed in real life, you can bring them into the matrimonial bed in your imagination – and without actually being unfaithful to or hurting your spouse.

Is this all right? Or does it do more harm than good? Is it worth replacing your spouse with thoughts of another person if it brings immediate gratification in your sexual life?

Do you know what goes on in your spouse's mind when you make love? When the lights go out and you press against each other's flesh, are you sure that it is your face they are seeing?

A few years ago I met a very friendly Jewish businessman who was happily married with children, but his wife was not Jewish. As time progressed he became more committed to his faith, and was anxious that his wife should think seriously about conversion. She was not as interested as he was and would need some convincing. When the three of us met to talk about the subject, I mentioned that it is absolutely forbidden in Judaism for a husband to think about another woman while making love to his wife, and vice versa. Until that moment, the businessman's wife had remained hostile to the idea of conversion. But now her eyes swelled with tears and her attitude was completely turned around.

She explained that although she trusted her husband's *physical* fidelity to her completely, as she aged she just did not know what was going through his *mind*. Was it the thought of one of his young employees that created passion in their bedroom? She told me, 'That law is the most beautiful thing I have ever heard. If this is what your religion is about, then I would like to become a Jewess right this very minute.'

Is a fantasy only a fantasy?

Just a few days after this heartening event, I related the gist of the story to a lawyer friend. He was not at all sympathetic. 'I would not be offended,' he told me, 'if my wife thought of someone else when we made love.

On the contrary, if that's the way she gets excited, then fine. It makes for greater passion in our marriage.'

'Yes,' I countered, 'but don't you feel that in such circumstances she would be making love not with *you*, but with a phantom, almost using you? Surely, it is not an experience you are both sharing.'

But he was emphatic. 'What goes on in my wife's heart of hearts is her business. So long as she remains loyal and loving in all the areas that I can overtly discern, I'm happy.'

Perhaps. But I have talked to many people who say they are deeply troubled by the possibility of their spouse secretly harbouring a strong sexual attraction to other people in general, and to a specific individual in particular. Most people view this kind of attraction in two ways, both of which are negative. First, they think it indicates a fault in themselves, whether sexually, physically, intellectually, or emotionally; and secondly, they take it as almost a kind of infidelity; an adultery of the mind, as it were. In the words of one woman who described her exasperation to me, 'If I am attractive, then why does my husband need to look at other women? The answer can only be that I am not as attractive as other women are. Hence, every time he looks intently at an attractive woman, I feel as though my own femininity has been stabbed and I wonder if he fantasises about her or me. I no longer feel like a woman.'

Here's another related question: is it OK to be turned on by men and women outside the marriage, and then use the excitement generated by staring at them to bring passion into marriage?

Once I was walking with my wife and my brother in

South Beach, the world-famous southern tip of Miami Beach, Florida, where I grew up. Today, it is the young people's capital of the world. Each night thousands of people revel, drink, and party there. The atmosphere is highly sexually charged and it goes without saying that a large percentage of the people are there to pick up or be picked up. I marvelled at the setting and said aloud that I did not know if this was the correct place for married couples to be.

My brother, who is certainly not a Rabbi, got upset. 'What's wrong with being here?' he asked me. 'There are many married couples who come here, and no doubt they do get turned on by many of the people who they see at the bars and walking up and down the strip. The women with low-cut blouses and short skirts. The men with their glorious muscles bulging out from their tight tank-top shirts and tight jeans. But this is all very productive and good. Couples come here, they get excited and feel sexy. And they go home and make love. Do you have anything against that?' he asked.

I thought long and hard. On the one hand, what harm is done? The husband and wife are there together, and they are experiencing the sights together. As long as they go home together, as opposed to with someone else, if their night out brings passion into their marriage, what harm has been done? On the contrary, this might even be said to have helped and enhanced their marriage – in which case, perhaps we should *encourage* husbands and wives to entertain thoughts of others while in the matrimonial bed!?

Stealing goodwill

In his list of 24 of the most unforgivable crimes in the Jewish religion, for which 'God will not allow the person who commits such deeds to repent because of the gravity of his transgression', Maimonides, the great 12th-century Jewish legalist and philosopher, includes the offence of *stealing goodwill*.

What does this mean? A modern-day version of one of Maimonides's examples might go something like this: Jack has just received a raise at work and has gone out and bought an expensive bottle of Dom Perignon champagne. Just as he arrives home with the intention of opening his bottle, he discovers that an old friend is calling on his doorstep. Jack hugs his friend, kisses him on the cheek, and tells him that he is ecstatically happy to see him, and that in his honour he will be opening an expensive bottle of Dom Perignon. He does, and by doing so he engenders a false sense of appreciation and love in his friend. He has stolen his friend's goodwill by performing an insincere and misleading gesture. His friend will walk away with a false sense of his own importance in his long-lost acquaintance's eyes.

A secret breach of trust

Adultery is not confined to a physically sexual affair or intercourse. To all intents and purposes, adultery takes place every time a husband or wife forms a strong emotional attachment to, and dependency on, a member of the opposite sex to whom they are not married – even if they never lay a finger on each other. The reason is that this constitutes an abuse of the marriage. A couple get married not just to have sex together, but to grow dependent on each other to the point where they become synthesised as one unit, albeit in two bodies. You get married not only because you are in love, but because you want to feel needed. Any emotional dependency on someone outside the marriage encroaches upon the couple's exclusive unity.

The ultimate form of stealing goodwill is when a husband or wife goes to bed with their spouse, engages in intimate and even passionate behaviour, yet all the time thinks about somebody else. Your spouse enjoys a special moment with you, you endeavour to give them pleasure and they walk away with a deeper feeling of love and attachment to you because of it, but it is an illusion, it is false. You didn't even think about them.

Making passionate love to your wife when really you are thinking about someone else, or even being turned on by someone else and then making passionate love to your wife when really you should be turned on by her, is a serious breach of trust. It is also one of the greatest forms of insult that we can offer to another human being, and one that people are not likely to forgive or forget easily. It is very detectable and discernible. There isn't a single man or woman in the world who does not know if their spouse is millions of miles away while they are in bed. The lovemaking is different and a big gap, a great distance, is felt. It simply cannot be concealed. Replacing your spouse with thoughts of someone else in human sexual relations is a grave sin and should be avoided in the very same way that adultery should be avoided.

After adultery: restoring trust

'My wife is a wonderful woman, but after twenty years of marriage she just doesn't light my fire the way she used to. So I dabble on the side. And who does it hurt anyway? I don't love any of them, and they're never really serious. My wife is the mother of my children and my companion for life. Why should she feel threatened by any of these temporary girlfriends?'

Does the man above sound strange to you? He shouldn't. All too many people are convinced of the same thing: they can have adulterous affairs, and it will have no effect on their marriage. But this just isn't so. If a couple does survive an adulterous affair, and even if their love for each other grows as a result of working together through the difficult times, it will not be without great cost and sacrifice.

The first casualty of adultery is the most severe of all: that of trust. Even if an unfaithful husband or wife swears that they will never again be unfaithful, and even if they are completely forgiven by their spouse with heartfelt sincerity, still the act will never be *forgotten*, and will always be a reminder to the betrayed spouse of what their partner is capable of doing. Face it, if it happened once it could happen again, and forgiving and forgetting are different things altogether.

Fits of paranoia

In the wake of adultery, it is inevitable that the offended spouse will succumb to paranoia. Every time the formerly adulterous partner is away from home their spouse will be anxious and nervous. What are they up to? I know that they swore it would never happen again. But it happened once before. Who are they meeting? These kinds of emotions will put severe strain on the marriage, because the spouse will be unusually nervous. They will speak to their partner in an unkind tone, and suspicions will be cast in all the wrong directions, making the partner feel unfairly trapped, and that the spouse's insecurities are too deep to deal with.

The offended spouse may not be able to discuss their anxieties with their partner, since they don't want to accuse then of something that may not even be happening, and look like an insecure and paranoid wreck. But in truth, it is the erring partner who has given rise to this paranoia. He or she may take offence at the many insinuations, but it is he or she who created them.

This invariably leads to the errant partner accusing their spouse of being irrational. The most innocent conversations will be suspected. Many arguments will ensue, and the partner ends up telling lies about innocent conversations, because the spouse does not see them as innocent.

This breakdown in communication is a shame, because one of the best ways to avoid adultery in marriage is for a husband and wife to have constant communication on the subject of sexual attraction to other men and women. A husband must be able to come home and speak with his wife honestly and directly about the secretary to whom he fears he may be getting too close, and the wife about the business associate with whom she has been working on an important project and perhaps spending too much time and allowing an unhealthy situation to develop. When these things can be discussed with total frankness and openness, then not only can adultery be averted, but greater honesty and trust can be brought into the marriage.

But what can one do when the once errant partner brings up the subject and the offended spouse immediately jumps down their throat? How can confidence be restored? The essential fact that adultery has been committed cannot be denied. There is no way out. There may be paranoia, but as the famous American baseball player Yogi Berra once said, 'Just because you're paranoid doesn't mean that they are *not* out to get you.'

One of the hallmarks of an adulterous affair is trust – particularly, trust that neither party will tell anyone else about the affair, unless they both agree on disclosure. Their trust induces a sense of togetherness and closeness, as if it is just them against all the world. Marriage must have at least this same degree of trust if it is to survive and flourish. A husband and wife need to feel confident that there are no secrets between them.

Love is impossible without respect

The loss of trust is coupled with another miserable consequence of adultery, namely, the loss of respect that one spouse has for the other. Of all the long-term effects of adultery, this is surely the most disastrous.

No wife can see the husband she once respected as a loyal spouse and adoring father in the same light after he has committed adultery. When she witnesses how every passing member of the opposite sex grabs his eye or how he flirts like an adolescent to the point of embarrassing himself, she perceives him as weak, uncommitted, and unable to control his life and shape his own destiny. In the final analysis, sexual infidelity is all about weakness. It means giving in to impulsive and selfish yearnings without any thought of how this submission will affect the lives of those whom we love most.

Why is respect so paramount in every relationship? For two reasons. The first has to do with the ephemeral quality of emotion. Whereas emotion is volatile, intellect is cool, calm and unchanging. In a thriving relationship, both intellect and emotion are necessary. No couple could happily stay together for intellectual reasons alone. Without love, there exists no glue, no attraction strong enough to keep a man and woman bound to each other. But emotion is fickle and fluctuating – the partner you love one moment, you may hate the next – and needs something more solid to ground it.

Respect based on an intellectual and moral appreciation of one's spouse provides a bedrock into which emotion can be anchored, as well as a spring whence emotion may flow out. If a husband and wife respect each other, the attraction between them will not easily come undone or fly away with the wind. When there is mutual respect, they don't merely love each other. Rather, they have a *reason* to love each other; their love is based on more than the feeling of *being in love*.

The other reason why respect is so vital is that it ends arguments. When one spouse respects the other they always find a reason to end an argument because they believe that their spouse must be right. When a husband, for example, fights with his wife whom he respects and looks up to as an honest, non-argumentative and humble individual, he will find it far easier to end the argument and apologise to his wife because he will assume that *she* is justified and that the reason for the argument lies with him. 'I'm just being stubborn,' he tells himself. Without this kind of respect, marital disputes would drone on endlessly with each spouse believing that they are correct and insisting that the other must capitulate.

It is easy to accept people we respect as our moral superiors. I believe that we find the existence of good, decent and honest people in our midst absolutely redeeming. They are like a breath of fresh air. Being married to a person whom we respect feels like a privilege, a privilege not easily forgotten even in the midst of battle. In this way respect prompts us to put an end to bouts of marital strife.

What adultery does, however, is not to erode this mutual respect gradually, as do ongoing marital altercations and bickering, but to destroy it in one fell swoop. The moment you hear that your spouse has been unfaithful, he or she becomes, in your eyes, not only an insensitive, uncaring weakling, but a stranger – not the good, honest person you thought you knew, but a *bad* person. Tragically, this can sound the death knell for any marriage.

Loss of trust

Of the many casualties of every act of infidelity, loss of trust is perhaps the most significant. Why? Because through every crisis in marriage, it is trust that pulls us through by allowing us to forgive and love in return. Even after a terrible row, if a husband tells his wife, 'Please forgive me because I really do love you and I didn't mean any of the things I said,' they can continue a normal and happy life together as long as she can still believe him.

But what if she can't? What if he doesn't tell the truth? What then is there to love? Everything the adulterer says is suspect. If he has a bad temper and calls his wife names, he can still apologise later, and she can accept it. But if he is dishonest, why should she accept his apology? Not everyone is as forgiving of catching their spouse in an adulterous affair as the Duc de Richelieu who, upon discovering his wife with her lover, said, '*Madame*, you must really be more careful. Suppose it had been someone else who found you like this?'

After a husband commits adultery, after he has led the duplicitous life which is necessary in an affair, after he has told two women simultaneously that he loves them, after he has shared the most intimate moments and the personal details of his life with someone who is not his wife, what is there to trust? Even if he apologises, his wife will not be able to forget that just last week he was telling her how much he loved *her*, but at the same time running around behind her back with someone else.

The road of return

One of the central tenets of the Jewish faith is that we can always repent and save a bad situation. We are never denied the road of return to our previous state of innocence. The belief that we are never beat, and life is never over, and that we can always reinvent ourselves regardless of our past, is the most important tenet of human living. It means that we are worthwhile and our lives are significant. So significant, that we can never be written off. Only death has the power to defeat us; there are no other excuses. You make a mistake, you pick yourself up and continue. The spiritual soul within us lends us an infinite capacity for life. And because it is pure, the dirt into which we immerse ourselves will never really stick. Even after an adulterous act, we can restore our marriage to its former state, and even make it better than before.

But it will require a bit of radical strategy.

Restoring trust

The love and trust that once existed in marriage can indeed be recaptured, and even built upon, after an act of infidelity. The secret lies in waiting, being patient and going to a temporary extreme.

The Jewish philosopher Maimonides discusses, in his treatise on human character, what a person should do if they have a very negative quality trait. First, he identifies what is a good quality trait, and what is evil. He basically says that any character trait that is extreme is evil, and can only be corrected by being brought into moderation. In fact, he goes as far as saying that the very definition of good and bad is moderation and extremism. Even too much of a so-called 'good' character trait is bad. We must find the golden middle path in each and every character trait and this will, in turn, bring us virtue.

But what if we are already extremists? The way forward charted by Maimonides is to go, temporarily, to the opposite extreme in order to compensate for one's imbalance, which will later lead to a state of moderation. So, for example, if you lose your temper too often, then you should strictly discipline yourself *never* to lose your temper for a while, thereby learning how to bring it under control.

In the case of restoring trust in a relationship after adultery, the way to undo the damage is for the adulterer to go to the opposite extreme: instead of showing a sexual interest in another person, they must show no attraction or feelings for another person whatsoever. This rule extends even to movie and pop idols. If you have been unfaithful, you need now to show your husband or your wife that you are interested in them, and them only, that no one else excites you in the slightest.

Therefore, when a wife suggests to her once errant husband that they go to the latest Madonna movie, I say in all seriousness that the husband's response should be that he has no interest in seeing it. Let him say, 'I don't find Madonna attractive. I love you, I don't need that.' And when his wife switches on a late-night movie, with explicit sexual scenes and nudity, he should turn over and read a book or go to sleep.

Lest I be accused of encouraging husbands to be dishonest with their wives about their sexual interests just in order to regain their confidence and trust, I must stress that this altered behaviour is crucial for the husband as well. It is not just his penance but his *therapy* to go to the opposite extreme for a certain duration and fight his attraction to others, even though this may be highly unnatural. The point is not that he should act synthetically *in order to fool his wife*. He is doing it for himself, to rid himself of a dangerous disposition. He is going to an extreme and making himself feel nothing for other women, even the most attractive, so that later he can find a healthy equilibrium where he notices his natural attraction to other women, yet controls his thoughts, speech and action, and focuses his sexual energy on his wife.

Begin with an effort

The benefits of this procedure are clear: the wife may not believe that her husband finds Kim Basinger boring and unattractive. She might also be incredulous about her husband's sudden loss of interest in television sex. However, she will definitely feel that, whether or not her husband is focusing all his attention on her and is bored by other women, *he is at least making a strong effort in that direction*.

Not only will his wife's paranoia subside, and her faith and confidence in him be slowly restored, but she will love him more than ever. She will see before her a man who undoubtedly stumbled, and caused more hurt to her than anything she has ever known. But she will also see a man who, despite his blunder, loves her with all his heart, and is prepared to make Herculean efforts to remain faithful and ensure that he never hurts her again. She will fall in love with her *new* husband, who struggles with a process of rebirth, and goes to a great extreme in order to assuage his wife's suffering, and restore her confidence that he will remain her loyal husband for ever more. And she will feel like the most wanted woman in the world.

How to stay in love

'I'm seriously looking for a wife and my friend Rob wanted me to take out his former girlfriend, Stacey. "She's a real screamer," he told me, "and a really nice girl." I subsequently heard from two other friends that they had taken her to bed, too. So I won't take her out. I don't want to compete with all the former men she has had, many of whom are far more handsome than me. I don't know that my ego can handle it. It just isn't nice.'

Why is it that we sometimes feel so dissatisfied with our spouse? We compare their looks and their actions with those of all the men and women who surround us and sometimes, inevitably, they are found wanting in comparison. We then use this deficiency to justify extramarital affairs, whether real or imagined. Can we learn to be more satisfied and appreciate what we have?

The very definition of love is subjectivity

I am convinced that one of the principal causes in the breakdown of relationships today is that we have become *objective* about the people we love. We've become objective about things that we were never meant to be objective about.

In seminars that I have conducted around the world
I have asked the members of the audience to posit a
one-word synonym for love. These are the most common responses: 'devotion', 'respect', 'admiration', and
'a longing' and finally 'selflessness'. These are all in-
sightful responses, but they somehow miss out the
essence of love. To me the best synonym for love is
subjectivity. Being in love with someone means not
seeing their faults, or being aware of their faults but
relegating them to the realm of insignificance. Your
love for them colours your perception of them, and *to
you* they appear beautiful and glorious, irrespective of
what the objective facts really are. 'This person is so
important, I know they have faults, but it does not
matter. To me, they are the most special person in the
world.'

Conversely, falling out of love is objectifying your
partner so that you are in a constant state of appraisal,
always comparing them with the people around you.
The breakdown in relationships is due to the fact that
we have become objective about the people we love.
We are constantly re-evaluating them as if to decide
whether they are still worthwhile, or whether perhaps
we made a mistake in marrying them.

A woman came to complain to me about her
husband. She said, 'To be honest, Rabbi, Jeffrey, who I
know from work, seems as though he would have been
a lot more suitable as a life-long partner. He's funnier,
more patient, loves kids, and is far more affectionate
than my husband. It's a pity that I didn't meet him five
years ago before I married.' It's easy to see how this
kind of attitude can lead directly to an adulterous affair.
Even after marriage, this woman is still comparing her

husband with everyone around her. She is still objective about her husband. So where is the love?

The most beautiful woman in the world

Contrast this woman's attitude with the following story. When I was a student in Rabbinical seminary, I was once invited to the home of an elderly couple for dinner by their grandson. During the meal, I dropped a fork under the table and bent down to pick it up. When I did, I noticed that this couple, both of whom were in their late seventies, were holding hands under the table. Coming as I did from a broken home, I was impressed; tears came to my eyes.

As I was leaving, I couldn't help but mention how happy I was to have witnessed this display of romantic love between the couple, and how their feelings for each other had not diminished through time. 'You are the world's greatest romantics,' I said. 'It's amazing!' The wife blushed at my words, but the husband did not. He just looked at me with a quizzical stare, as if he did not really understand me. 'You sound surprised that we can remain in love for all these years. Why, for me it's very easy. After all, my wife is the most beautiful woman in the whole wide world,' and he kissed her as he said this.

What amazed me was that his sincerity was beyond question. I couldn't believe it. He was completely sincere and it showed. Why was I surprised? Because it was blatantly not true! Surely, however attractive his wife was, I didn't expect to wake up the next morning and find her face on the cover of *Vogue*! In fact, *objectively* speaking she looked as though she was 900 years old and had so many chins that I couldn't even count them.

And yet, not only did he mean every word, but also he was accurate. What he was saying was this: *to me*, she is the most attractive woman in the world. I love her and therefore I am subjective in my evaluation of her. I don't want anyone else. Just her. No one else's personal opinion of his wife mattered. In his world, in his realm of experience, she was the most glamorous woman alive. And this is the way things ought to be. A man and a woman should indeed view their spouse as the most special, most beautiful person on the planet. A husband and wife's love for each other should alter the very way in which they perceive each other.

If this does not happen, then there is something missing, something inadequate, in their love. If you disagree and feel that this is too high a standard, then consider how you would feel about a parent who thought their child ugly or stupid, even if it were true. Would you applaud their honesty? No, you would probably be horrified.

The fact is that every parent thinks that his or her child is the cleverest and most precious in the galaxy, and every one of them is absolutely right.

Has it ever happened that you are patiently sitting in a doctor's waiting room, and someone's kid doesn't stop crying, sneezing on you, staring at the inside of your nostrils, and generally making you wish that you could strangle him and put everyone in the waiting room out of their misery? Then, just as you finish tying the noose to do the dirty deed, you see the child's mother looking starry-eyed at her son, as she says, looking right at you, 'Isn't he adorable? He's so sweet!'

Of course, it's blatantly untrue. But the love which a mother has for her child is capable of transforming a monster into an angel, at least in her own eyes.

Now, we seem to accept that this should be true of children. Why don't we accept that the same should be true of our partners in relationships and marriage? Why aren't we as subjective? Everyone of us is perfectly capable of cheating on our spouse in a way that we would never betray our children. The reason: whereas we might compare our children with other children, but still never find ourselves seriously dissatisfied with them, the same is not true of our spouse. Husbands and wives are evaluating each other constantly, with adultery the direct outcome.

A husband may look upon his ageing wife and compare her with a younger woman in much the same way that he compares his 1990 Sony Walkman with the newer, more feature-laden edition. And just as he sells the old Walkman to buy the new model, he can trade his wife in for a newer model, either through divorce, or, an apparently far less messy solution, by having an affair.

Searching for 'the best'

In marriage, each one of us is not interested in someone who is good enough, and suits all of our needs and desires. What we want today is *the best*. I cannot begin to relate how many times I have heard young successful people justify breaking off relationships with men and women with whom they were once very serious, not because of any real problem, but simply because, in their estimation, they did not reach their high standards. What they want is the best, so they will keep looking.

What we forget is that, while we can speak of the plushest house, the fanciest car or the finest cigar, because they are superficial material objects, we cannot speak of 'the best' person because every human being has infinite depth and is special in their own different way. No wonder, then, that we often go out with the wrong person since we do not seek someone who suits us, so much as someone who is judged to be 'the best' according to values that are arbitrary and shallow. Sometimes I really think that if a woman could have a CD player with speakers implanted into her hip, this would be viewed by a man as another reason to marry her. In addition to her heart and soul, she also comes along with a hi-fi system! That's how superficial things have become as we elusively pursue 'the best'.

But there is no such thing as 'the best' in marriage; there is nothing better than *good enough*. We should treat marriage like a glove that fits. The person who makes us happy and whom we miss when they are not around, and who seeks to make us happy and fulfils all our needs, is the one who is usually perfectly suited to us. But people often refrain from marrying such a person, especially if they are one of the first people they date, since they feel they *must* first shop around, see who else is available, because maybe it will turn out that while this person is *good*, they are not *the best*.

The wife I married was, thank God, the very first girl I dated, and when I tell this to our students at Oxford they look very surprised. 'Look, Debbie is a great wife,' they admit, 'but could you have been sure that she was the right girl for you if you had no one to compare her with?' And armed with this philosophy, the students date and date in search of the very best possible partner for life, and in the process ensure that no one will make them happy since it is not human warmth they seek, but accolades.

If this approach to relationships were confined to the time before marriage, it would be forgivable. The problem is that once you teach yourself to objectify people, it won't stop even after you marry: you will fail to find satisfaction with your spouse since you will still be scrutinising your other acquaintances to see if you could have done better.

Marriage means choosing one partner for life, and closing off all other possibilities. The search has now been terminated.

Love means being utterly subjective. This is not something negative, for it means focusing on essence. It means transcending cosmetic and superficial layers and concentrating on the deepest, most special part of a person, the part of them that cannot be assessed or appraised. This kind of deep love is not instantaneous; it can be achieved only through sharing, living and striving together, and through extraordinary commitment and sacrifice: primarily through marriage.

Premarital sex and marriage

One of the greatest obstacles to this penetrating love is when people engage in extensive sexual relations before marriage. Statistics show that the rate of divorce increases exponentially with the number of sexual partners and the amount of sexual experience one has before marriage.

This is borne out logically as well. If we engage in numerous relationships, and come to know many people intimately, later when we marry we will begin to compare our spouses with the people we knew so well before. How could we not? We will see that they don't measure up, because no one is so multi-faceted that they could possibly embrace every human attribute that can be pooled among so many various partners.

I will never forget how once, a couple came to see me to patch up their marriage after the wife's infidelity. She loved her husband, but felt that she could not now enjoy him after her affair. 'Why?' I asked. 'Is it because you feel guilty?' '*Not at all*,' she said, in her husband's presence. 'The other man's "equipment" was better, and therefore I enjoyed it more. And it's difficult to go back to my husband.'

Having many sexual partners before marriage and many intimate relationships leads us to the single most destructive force in marriage: objectivity. People cannot be compared. Our spouse, who should be the most special person in the world to us, becomes a number on a scale, rated by comparison with others we have known. This kind of thinking is demoralising and dehumanising.

If you have been intimate with many partners before marriage, it will take great discipline to focus your mind on your spouse. You must slowly allow the strong images of the past to fade by not focusing on them ever. You must dismiss these images whenever they are conjured up in your mind. Banish them from your thoughts. Don't allow them to encroach on the intimacy you seek with your spouse. This intimacy is the secret of a satisfying and passionate sexual life in marriage.

But it can be severely and adversely affected if something creeps into the bedroom with you, especially
something like the thought of another person with
whom the very same experiences were shared pre-
viously. When the thought of other partners creeps in,
can the experience be said to be intimate?

The ghosts of lovers past

What makes something special is the fact that it is
distinct and unique. In Jewish thought the very word
'holy' means 'separate, distinct, and different'. The
Sabbath day is holy by virtue of the fact that it is
different from the other days of the week, and it is
treated differently. If one treats it in exactly the same
way as one treats Tuesday, if one goes to work and
drives the car, then it stops being special.

The same applies to intimacy. What makes a sexual
moment exciting and special is the fact that it is only
the two of you who experience it. But when the ghosts
of former lovers enter your minds, the whole experience suffers.

This is especially true because of the very physical
nature of human sexuality. Memories are strong
enough when they involve a conversation, a laugh, an
emotional exchange. But they are positively stifling
when they involve intense physical pleasure, excitement and fulfilment. Inevitably, if one brings such
memories into the bedroom, one will be tempted to
judge the performance of one's current partner by
comparison.

I strongly advise against informing your fiancé(e),
or your spouse, of sexual liaisons – boyfriends,

girlfriends, one-night stands and so on – that took place before you met your current partner. You have to allow those previous images, however powerful, to fade, and the most effective way of doing this is never to discuss them. It is simply none of their business, and even if they want to know, don't indulge their curiosity. It doesn't increase trust or faithfulness. It can bring nothing but unnecessary hurt. Worse still, those memories might lead you to compare your current happiness and satisfaction with that experienced in a previous relationship. So why allow this to become a subject of conversation? It is imperative that a husband and wife begin life anew. They should not bring the ghosts of relationships past into their marriage.

Love in marriage

Love means the ability to lose objectivity, to forget the insignificant, ancillary, and shallow details of a man or woman, instead choosing to embrace their core. A person's infinite soul, when allowed to shine forth through all its transient coverings, becomes truly fulfilling and powerful enough to sustain everlasting human excitement and commitment.

SOURCES

Carol Botwin, *Tempted Women*, 1994, William Morrow & Co., quoted on pp. 30, 70, 154–5

Naura Hayden, *How to Satisfy a Woman Every Time*, 1982, Biblio O'Phile Publishing Co., quoted on pp. 31–2, 144

Dalma Heyn, *The Erotic Silence of the American Wife*, 1993, Turtle Bay Books, quoted on p. 55–6

Shere Hite, *The Hite Report*, 1987, Ballantine, quoted on pp. 51, 53, 55, 80, 164–5; *The Hite Report on Love, Passion and Emotional Violence*, 1991, quoted on p. 20

Independent on Sunday, 16 January 1994, quoted on p. 21

The Janus Report on Sexual Behaviour, 1993, John Wiley & Sons, Inc., quoted on pp. 18, 23

Tony Lake & Ann Hills, *Affairs*, 1979, quoted on p. 78–9

Masters and Johnson, *Sex and the Art of Human Loving*, 1985, quoted on pp. 141–2, 142, 143

Bertrand Russell, *Why I Am Not a Christian*, 1957, quoted on p. 122; *Autobiography Vol. I*, 1967, quoted on p. 122

George Bernard Shaw, *Man and Superman*, 1903, quoted on p. 42

Sunday Times, 11 April 1993, quoted on pp. 104, 105

Kathleen Tait, *My Father Bertrand Russell*, 1976, quoted on p. 122

Talmud, Avod a Zarah 18b and Kedushin 80b, quoted on p. 148–9, 149–50